FRIENDLY REFUGE

To the friendly people of Malta

FRIENDLY REFUGE

GEORGE. H. MUSGRAVE

George Musgrave

HEATHFIELD PUBLICATIONS
STATION RD.,
HEATHFIELD, Sussex

First published 1979.

ISBN 0 9506480 0 0

Published by: Heathfield Publications,
Station Road, Heathfield, Sussex.

Printed by: Ashdown Press, South View Road,
Crowborough, Sussex.

Distributed exclusively in Malta by
Progress Press Company Limited,
341, St. Paul Street, Valetta, Malta.

CONTENTS

ILLUSTRATIONS

ACKNOWLEDGMENTS

How many readers when they reach the end of a book spend time examining the Bibliography? The reason I have included one is because I am grateful to the people who wrote the books I have listed. They all added something to my knowledge as, over a period of four years, I have searched for clues that would help to build up as accurate an account as possible of what happened in Malta in AD 60. Few of the listed books make any mention of Malta but each dealt with issues relevant to my theme. I am grateful to George Allen & Unwin for permission to quote from Lionel Casson's 'Travel in the Roman World' which I found particularly instructive.

I cannot claim to be an archaeologist. It was therefore of immense value to me to find such ready help from experts in this field. Professor John Evans, Principle of the Archaeological Institute, London, generously gave his time over a long period and I also value the help and encouragement of Dr. David Whitehouse, Director of the British School at Rome who also went to the trouble of photographing for me the painting of St. Paul's shipwreck at S. Paolo fuori le Mura and I am grateful for the ready permission of that Church.

Within Malta I found much help. I am indebted to Dr. A. Bonano, Professor of Archaeology at the University of Malta for permission to reproduce the Salina Bay catacomb photographs on pages 73, 78, 79 & 87 which he took for me and to Denis de Luca for his on-the-spot help and surveying. (pages 74, 75 and part of 89.) Needless to say, the conclusions I reach in the following pages are not necessarily shared by those mentioned above.

Gathering together the fruits of exploration and much study lead inevitably to the discipline of condensing much material and here my thanks are due to members of my family and friends who gave much time to critical analysis. Particularly must I mention the Rev. Eric Burton who spent many hours editing and raising issues of value. Nor do I forget Linda Williams, Marion Parsons and Geraldine Hatton who spent tedious hours at the typewriter in various stages of preparing, revising and presenting the manuscript.

Having started by drawing attention to the Bibliography at the end I now have another unusual suggestion to make. If any readers are not familiar with the narrative of the shipwreck of St. Paul as described in chapters 27 and 28 of the Acts of the Apostles I recommend that you read it before commencing to read this book. For your convenience I have reproduced the story at the end using a modern translation, viz: from the Good News Bible. I am obliged to Collins Ltd and the British and Foreign Bible Society for permission to include it. With easy access to the original story it should enable the reader to check the clues discussed in the ensuing pages.

INTRODUCTION

My interest from the beginning was to write a novel about St. Paul in whom I have had a great interest since my youth. From the outset I was concerned to seek as accurate a presentation as possible. The deeper my researches the more I felt my unreadiness for the task. Malta drew my attention to a number of issues that I felt deserved special attention. The following pages are an attempt to deal with some of them. The novel must come later.

Some readers may not agree with all the conclusions reached. Some may not want to. But this book is an honest attempt to find the truth about what happened when Paul came to Malta and the years which immediately followed. I do not believe this has been previously attempted in quite the form that this book takes. For my own part the task was most rewarding.

If some of my conclusions seem presumptuous I can only claim that they are reached after very considerable research and deliberation. My interest is the search for truth.

The passing of centuries has caused so much evidence to disappear. Here and there folk tales have embroidered fragments of fact lost in the mists of time. We wish we could be sure of much that is tantalizingly vague. We wish the next upturned stone would reveal some undeniable evidence.

We cannot expect farmers to be archaeologists. Over the centuries ancient sites have become obliterated because succeeding generations have had no interest in ruins beyond the readily available building material which they provide.

The interest of the farmer, quite rightly, was to make the best use of his fields. If stones were impeding his plough they were best removed. If there was a hole in the ground it was an ideal receptacle for debris. Gradually traces of former civilizations have disappeared. It is only with much patience, careful searching, deduction and sometimes even inspiration that one is able to detect clues which help us to discover and analyse sites where people of a forgotten age once lived.

Writing this book has been an exciting experience as one by one fresh pieces of evidence presented themselves to me. Again and again I have gone back to Malta to search anew. I hope many readers will do the same.

ACROSS THE GREAT SEA

Myra is in southern Turkey. When Paul was there it was a flourishing port. It was the last dry land upon which he stood before the fateful voyage which brought him to Malta. When visiting the places which had been the scenes of his missionary ventures this was one place I particularly wanted to see.

Most knowledgeable people whose advice I sought shook their heads and implied that it was too inaccessible a location to reach overland because of the mountains. I am glad I made the tiring but exciting trip for it has left me with vivid memories for I was able to gain some conception of what this ancient port was like when Paul made his brief stay there over nineteen hundred years ago.

An English geologist I met on the journey over the mountains warned me, "You know, of course, that there are bears in these parts? Last month a pack of wolves raided a village and carried off all the sheep. You need to keep your eyes open for snakes, too. But the thing you need to look out for most of all are the scorpions. They are about six inches long and very dangerous. I always carry a stick with me."

We parted company near the sea at Finike. Before he went on his way I obtained the help of his limited Turkish to enable me to share a ramshackle conveyance meant for four. My companions were six Turks and their considerable baggage! It was a hair-raising trip along the narrow coast road cut out of the cliff face. At every hairpin bend there were sheer drops of fifty feet or more to the hungry sea below. Nobody spoke English. The only Turkish I knew was Merhaba (hello).

Arriving at the end of the route I walked the last mile or two alone and found myself amid the silence of the ancient ruins of Myra. In the satisfaction of having reached an objective and with some useful pictures taken, my conversation with the geologist was already forgotten. Suddenly, as I was in the process of clearing a path through the tangled thorns and undergrowth near to one of the side entrances of the huge Theatre, I heard a steady movement closeby. The noise steadily drew nearer. I stood still and held my breath. There could be no doubt about the sound of the breaking of twigs. Something was moving towards me. Remembering the geologist's advice I quickly looked around for a stick but could see nothing that would be of use. The noise sounded closer and closer. Suddenly a gap appeared in the undergrowth little more than a yard away. To my relief I saw that the cause of the disturbance was a giant tortoise!

As I stood beside the ancient Theatre at Myra this trifling incident put my mission in perspective. What for me was a sight-seeing and fact-finding visit had been for Paul yet one more milestone on a painful, often frustrating and heavy-hearted journey, leading inevitably to martyrdom for his faith. His body already carried many scars. More devastating experiences were yet to come. He had probably stood near to where I was standing at that moment.

Nearby would have been the quayside, for in those days the inlet, now silted up long since, used to reach close to the high rocky cliffs which towered above the Theatre. There in the shelter of those cliffs would be the ship bound for Andramyttium which had brought him from Caesarea. Soon he was to step aboard the doomed corn-ship just arrived from Egypt and scheduled to carry its precious cargo to Rome.

Lionel Casson in his 'Travel in the Ancient World' has graphically sketched for us the sailing conditions of those days pointing out that the main function of vessels was to carry cargo.

Passengers who were allowed to travel were granted few facilities. They had to prepare their own food and bring their own pots and pans and mattresses. The provision of cabins was so rare that most had to sleep on the deck in tentlike structures erected nightly. People had to take their turn at the cooking-hearth in the galley and many were glad to have servants with them to attend to the chores.

Passengers had to wait ashore until they heard the cry of the herald making his rounds, announcing the departure of the vessel. The time of sailing depended on many factors. Because the ships relied upon sail it was necessary for the wind to be in the right direction. Because superstition was rife there were other things which had to be taken into consideration before a skipper would feel happy about sailing, including the date! As Lionel Casson puts it:

> "Assuming that the wind was favourable and there was nothing wrong with the date, the ship's authorities would proceed to make a pre-sailing sacrifice (a sheep or a bull; Poseidon preferred bulls), and, if the omens during this were not right, the sailing had to be delayed. If the wind was favourable, if there was nothing wrong with the date, and if the sacrifice had gone off as desired, superstition still left a gamut of bad omens to be run: a sneeze as you went up the gangplank was bad (although if you had sneezed to the right during the sacrifice, that was good), a crow or a magpie sitting, croaking, in the rigging was bad, a glimpse of some wreckage on the shore was bad, the uttering of certain words or expressions was bad."

From the above we can gain some conception of the grip which superstition had on the minds of many in that generation and the delays to schedule which could result from this factor alone.

How long Paul was in Myra is not clear. We only know that as a result of the decision of the Roman centurion Julius, in charge of the group of prisoners which included Paul, they changed ship here. It was a decision which was to be of vital significance to the people of Malta. To get to Rome by the overland route before winter was out of the question. It would take Imperial couriers something like fifty days and these were specially trained men. To get a motley group of prisoners over numerous mountain ranges before the snows blocked them, was asking for trouble.

We live in a generation that has forgotten the sailing ship as a vehicle of commerce. We have watched the disappearance of steamships and the development of oil-burning monsters. Sailing ships are now virtually confined to small craft designed for leisure purposes close to the shore. In Paul's day, apart from the smaller coastal fishing boats, there were large cargo ships built specifically for trade across the Mediterranean. Julius was faced with the problem of the late season. The normally accepted period for sailing was almost at an end. Ships did not cross the Great Sea between November and March, the Feast of Tabernacles marking the end of the safe period of navigation. This tradition was partly because of unsuitable sailing conditions but chiefly because before the days of the compass Mariners relied upon sun and stars to plot their course. It was a risky business. Paul advised against the voyage but was ignored.

For over two years after his arrest on a trumped-up charge in Jerusalem Paul had been a prisoner at Caesarea. Felix, the first Roman governor who had tried him, might have released him if Paul had agreed to pay a handsome enough bribe. The next governor, Festus, did not believe Paul to be guilty and implied that he would have let him go free had he not chosen to be tried before Caesar.

That there were other prisoners beside Paul is clear and the squad of soldiers under the command of the centurion Julius probably numbered about twelve. Presumably these soldiers, as well as Julius, were of the Augustan cohort who appear to have been picked and trained men to whom special guard assignments were given.

So the disastrous voyage began. Vividly Luke has described it in Chapters 27 and 28 of the Acts of the Apostles. So we come to Malta.

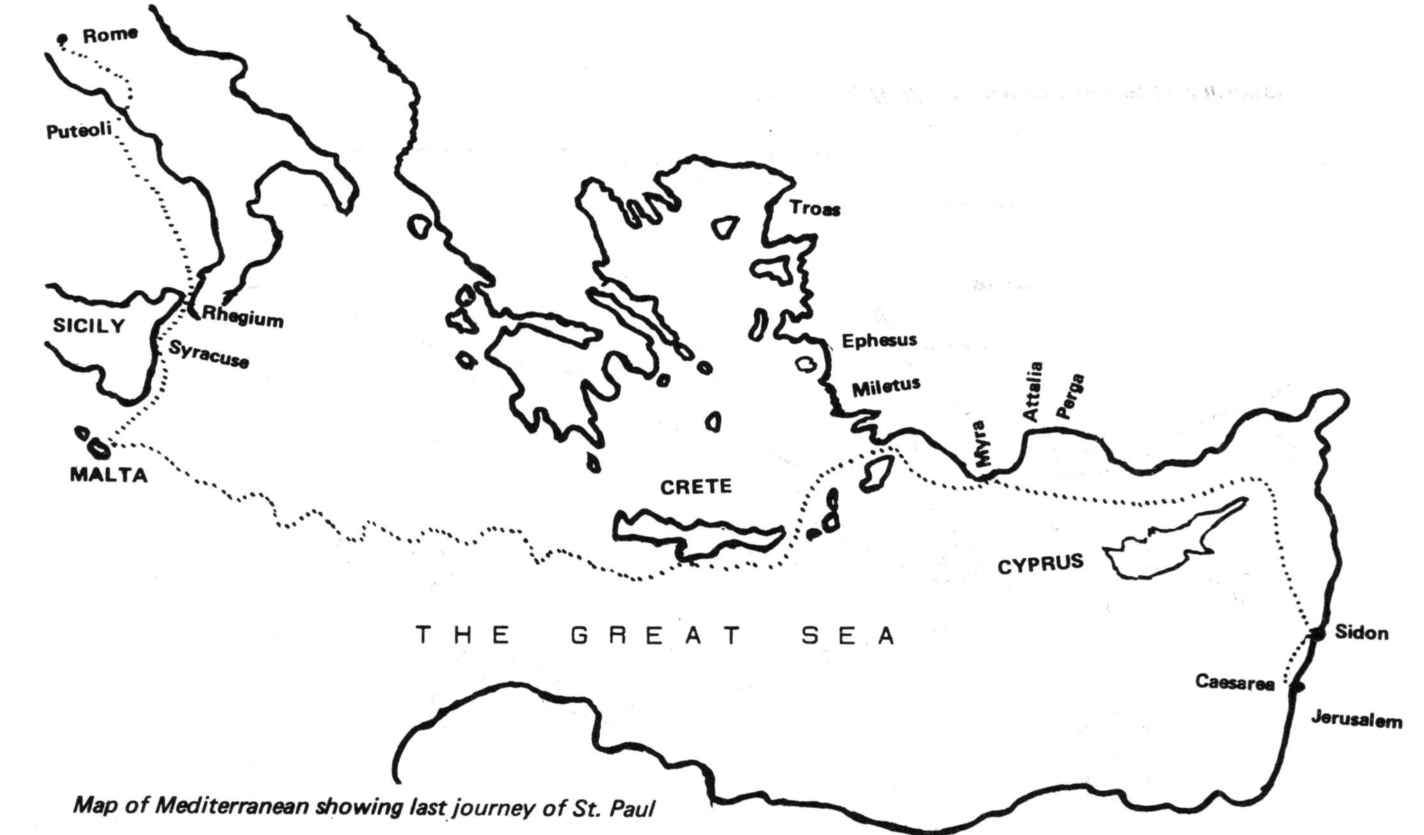

Map of Mediterranean showing last journey of St. Paul

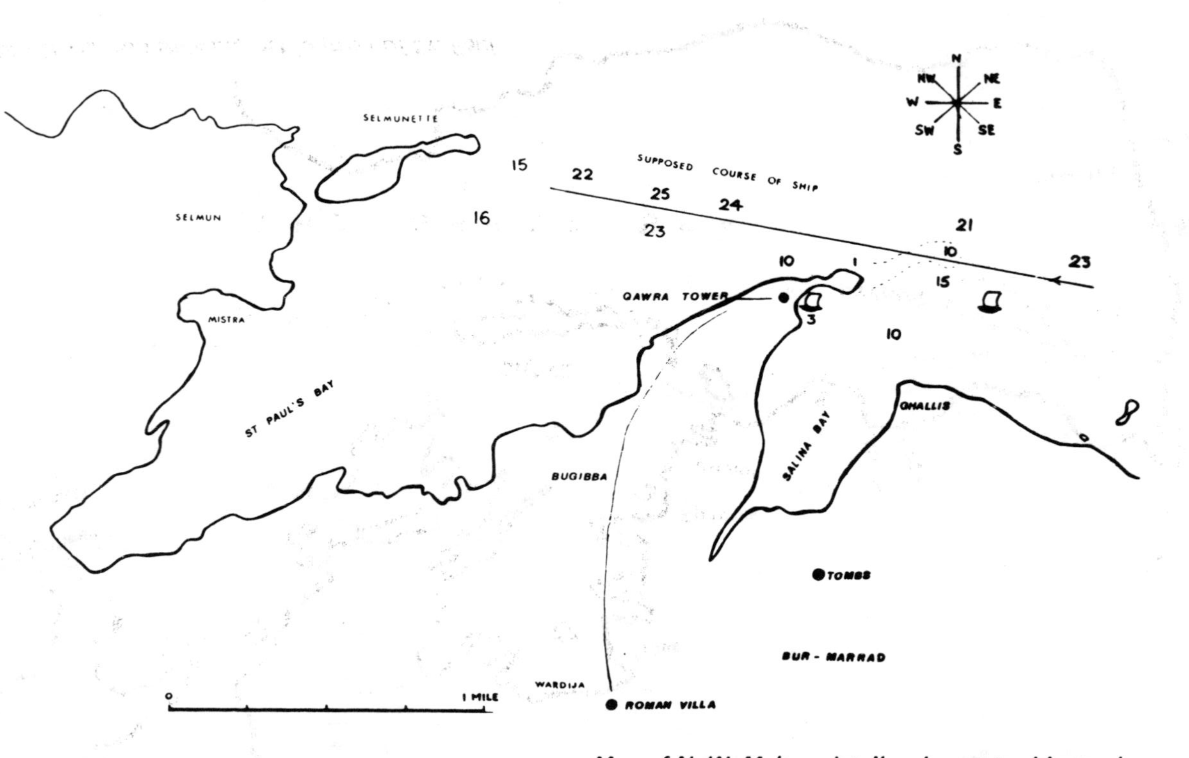

Map of N. W. Malta: details relevant to shipwreck.

SEARCHING FOR SHIPWRECK CLUES

On the islands of Selmunette at the entrance to St. Paul's Bay, stands the memorial to St. Paul. It was erected in the nineteenth century. The reason it was put there was because a tremendous stir had been caused by the remarkable book written by Capt. J. Smith 'The Voyage and shipwreck of St. Paul.' He maintained that the ship anchored off Qawra, was wrecked off Selmunette and that the survivors swam ashore at Mistra. In recent years a number of writers have questioned the theory. Among them, Dr. Burridge in 1952 in his 'Seeking the site of St. Paul's shipwreck' suggested Mellieha on the extreme west coast of Malta. It is significant, however, that long before Smith's impressive book, centuries of tradition have associated the shipwreck with the bay that today bears his name.

I began to have my doubts about the traditional site when one afternoon in November 1974 my wife and I walked along the clifftops of Selmun until, buffetted by the strong wind, we looked across the angry sea to the islands of Selmunette. From the bleak cliffs we looked down at the waves crashing on the rocks below and realised that this spot offered little hope of a landing place. We realised what a terrible experience it must have been to stand on the deck of a Roman sailing ship in the process of being dashed to pieces in such a setting. On that exposed rock we felt the power of the gregale (the north east wind). It was obvious that the ship could not have been wrecked on the islands themselves for if the terrified travellers had scrambled ashore there they would have had to be rescued by boat, for a stretch of water separates them from the main island. The narrative rules this out.

If the ship had struck close to the islands the distance to the beach at Mistra was too far to expect exhausted people to get safely ashore even if they were strong swimmers. We have to remember the following. They had been without food for a long period. Immediately before the ship was wrecked they had unloaded a heavy corn cargo which must have taxed their strength to the limit. There was a gale blowing. Many could not swim at all. Yet all two hundred and seventy six got safely ashore! From Selmunette to Mistra beach would have taken a long time for a strong swimmer in the peak of condition. For the slowest and weakest it would have taken hours – if possible at all. Somehow this did not seem to be the right location.

Hours spent poring over the oldest maps and records at the National Museum in Valletta produced the evidence that, whereas they all associate the shipwreck of St. Paul with the bay that now bears his name, it was not until Smith's book that attention was drawn to the western side of the bay. Earlier tradition makes no claims for his part of the bay. The earliest evidence of a Christian church is to be found on the eastern side of the bay at Bugibba.

To read Capt. Smith's masterly book, rich in seaman's knowledge of sailing ships, is a fascinating experience. Convincingly he demonstrates that the voyage from Myra would have brought the doomed ship to the north west coast of Malta, to roughly a quarter of a mile from Qawra point. I will not attempt to reproduce his convincing analysis. It has long been generally accepted.

My starting point, and where my reasoning leads me to conclusions different from his, is the arrival of the ship off Malta after fourteen days of a storm so devastating that it had been necessary to undergird the ship to hold leaking planks together and to jettison the loose tackle. They had not eaten, or had been unable to eat, for much of the period of the gale. They had no idea where they were because they had seen neither sun nor star (their means of charting their course) for most of the voyage. Their main fear was they they might at any time be wrecked on the Syrtis, treacherous sands off Africa. It was night-time and they were still being driven by the storm. About midnight on that fourteenth night the intuition of the sailors led them to suspect that land was near, presumably sight or sound of breakers on rocks. Capt. Smith believed this to be Qawra. I believe it was Ghallis.

Capt. Smith produced a map indicating the supposed course of the ship and indicating the depth of the sea off St. Paul's Bay to support his theory. In the map on page I have reproduced the figures he used but have supplemented his information with additional depths from modern maps. Below eleven fathoms the figures indicate feet. Remembering that the original narrative tells us that soundings were taken at twenty fathoms and shortly after at fifteen fathoms after which the anchors were dropped, we see that these conditions are met both off Qawra and Ghallis.

There is an extensive under-water reef off Qawra. It is important, therefore, to give consideration to the size of the ship involved. It was almost certainly a 'round ship' with a length-to-beam ratio of about four to one, which was common for merchant ships of the day. An Alexandrian corn ship described by Lucian in his dialogue 'The Ship, or human wishes' and written in the second century AD, gives a length overall of 182 feet, beam more than 45 feet and height from deck to bilges of 44 feet, with an estimated cargo of 1200 tons. Some four hundred years earlier King Hiero II, king of Syracuse, had a ship of nearly 1800 tons with over two hundred sailors aboard. Most merchant ships were considerably smaller than this with 400-500 tons burden being commonplace. Some idea of the cargo these ancient ships were capable of carrying can be realised when one visits the Bardo Museum in Tunis, where it takes several rooms to display the contents of a ship wrecked off Mahdia (the Syrtis so feared by mariners of the ancient world) in 81 BC. Amongst many fascinating items are two wonderfully preserved wooden beds beautifully shaped, obviously on their way to adorn some colonial villa.

We can only guess at what size Paul's ship was. We have to bear in mind that there were 276 people aboard and this factor alone would require considerable deck space for sleeping. Dr. Burridge suggests 180 feet by 40 feet. Capt. Smith calculates the length to have been about 100 feet, width about 25 feet and about 1200 tons. With such a size, it is questionable whether a ship almost certainly low in the water with a waterlogged corn cargo, could have got safely across the underwater reef at Qawra along the line of the supposed route indicated on his map, which I have reproduced on mine. (page 18)

That the ship was waterlogged is clear from the fact that tackling had already been thrown overboard to lighten it. Because the planks were coming apart they had found it necessary to undergird the ship with cables to pull them together. Smith himself pointed out that on the course the ship was sailing it was impossible to enter St. Paul's Bay without passing within a quarter of a mile of Qawra point, which, in view of the underwater reef, allows very narrow limits for his theory. Assuming that this hazard had been avoided we now have to meet, step by step, the requirements of the rest of the original narrative.

It was night-time when they had dropped the four anchors from the stern and spent the next few hours of darkness in sleepless anxiety. Their situation was made worse by the loss of the boat which the soldiers had cut adrift, when it was suspected that the sailors were about to desert to save their own skins. This incident proves that the sailors believed themselves to be near enough to shore for them to think that they had a better chance with the boat. The comment of Paul "unless these men stay aboard you can none of you come off safely", implies that the events of the next day were going to demand qualities of seamanship that only the sailors could provide. Daylight brought a gleam of hope. They were outside a bay of some sort. It was just possible that they might be able to thrust into it. There seemed a large element of doubt. It would need all the skills of the seamen to accomplish it. If they were off Qawra, on the fifteen fathom line, with a north east wind blowing, they would be potentially already inside St. Paul's Bay and should not have had much doubt about their ability to thrust the ship in. But they did have doubt!

With this doubt about the point of anchorage, let us now examine in detail just what the occupants of the ship saw when daylight came. To do so we must consider some of the alternative translations from the original Greek:

"They discovered a certain creek with a shore" (Authorised)
"They perceived a bay with a sandy beach" (Revised)
"They noticed a bay with a sandy beach" (New English Bible)

"noticed a creek with a sandy beach" (Moffat)
"An inlet with a sandy beach attracted their attention" (Weymouth)
"They could make out a kind of bay with a beach" (Jerusalem Bible)
"bay with a shelving beach" (Hastings Dictionary of the Bible)
"They could see a small bay with a sandy beach" (New World – Alan Dale)

The common denominator of all the translations is, that shelter from the open sea was potentially available and that there was land low enough to run the ship aground which could be a beach, sandy or otherwise, or an inlet or creek. There is sand at Mistra in St. Paul's Bay. There is sand at the mouth of the creek in Salina Bay. In the case of the latter it can be clearly seen from the fifteen fathom mark. The sand at Mistra could not be recognised as such unless the ship had already moved far into the bay to below fifteen fathoms. From such a position we could not consider the islands as the location for the wreck! We have already discussed the problem of negotiating Qawra reef to get to the fifteen fathom line in St. Paul's Bay. A ship anchored off Qawra, whether close in or half a mile out would see two bays. Any of the above translations would be consistent with a ship anchored off Ghallis.

Dunstan Bellanti in his book 'Why Malta? Why Chawdex?" says that the word 'Mistra' is derived from the Arabic adjective Mistur (hidden) and testor (to conceal). Mistra beach could hardly have been seen from a ship wrecked off the islands or further out before it was wrecked. A mile or rocky cliffs with a storm raging would have filled the strongest swimmer with despair.

Today there are salt pans in Salina Bay. These were not there in Roman times. They were developed in the days of the Knights. Prior to this there was a creek where the salt pans now are. Some writers have suggested that it stretched inland as far as Wardija. Realising that in Roman times both a creek and a beach existed this bay seems to fit all the requirements of the various translations better than St. Paul's Bay.

Let us search further in deciding what the anxious travellers did or did not see when day dawned. The writer of the narrative gives no indication that as their eyes searched the coastline they saw any sign of human habitation to cheer them; no word of houses or huts or of ships at anchor in a friendly harbour; no smoke of fires; no sign of people or domestic animals. Yet, later in the day, natives were to come to their aid. We know of at least one man-made feature which existed at that time and should easily have been seen from the deck of a ship at the mouth of St. Paul's Bay. At the eastern side of the bay was a neolithic temple which had already been there more than a thousand years. Today it is hidden by the buildings of a modern hotel named 'Dolmen' after the ruin which was once a landmark. In AD60 it would have been conspicuous from a ship within St. Paul's Bay. Perhaps the rain rendered the visibility poor. If so, this further dismisses the possibility of discerning a beach at Mistra from the deck of a ship considerably more than a mile away.

All the translations give the impression that the viewer saw the creek and shore quite clearly as though it was not at too great a distance. Later in the narrative we again come across the importance of the distance from ship to shore. When the ship had run aground the soldiers suggested that the prisoners should be killed. They feared that some might swim away and gain their freedom. With the prospect of a long swim across the bay to Mistra this was hardly likely to enter their heads, but it was a real likelihood if the ship ran aground some fifty yards south of Qawra!

For the time being let us leave the question of distances and consider the course of events, the time factor.

When the daylight was strong enough for them to survey the coast decisions had to be made. That the time was spent in discussion, possibly argument, is apparent by the doubts involved in the phrase 'if possible'. It was a question of seamenship, a question of how much sail to use bearing in mind the wind direction and its strength in relation to the shore now visible. It was a question of judgement regarding the use of the rudder-oars and anchors. All these would be discussed and it would take time. It would also have taken the crew and passengers many hours to bring up the cargo of sodden wheat from below decks and to throw it overboard. For exhausted men this would be a slow job. After a fortnight of fasting and terror they would be very tired men when the orders were at last given to cut away the anchors. It was probably midday before the order was given to abandon ship. It would have been quite a while after this before the last of the non-swimming voyagers had dared to jump into the sea and, grasping their planks, struggled ashore. To consider Mistra as the landing place would be to contemplate an extremely long swim. We would have to allow several hours before the last survivor was helped ashore. Time has to be allowed for lighting a fire with wet sticks which first had to be searched for and assembled. Luke vividly describes the episode of the snake bite and goes out of his way to mention that the natives, who by now had arrived to assist the travellers, watched 'a long time' expecting Paul to die from the bite. From the above we must assume that by now the afternoon was well advanced. Apart from all else, exhausted men would require a fairly prolonged rest period before they were ready to attempt further physical exertion. The longer and more exhausting the swim the more time we must allow for recovery. It would have to be a pretty late start before walking to the accommodation provided by the Chief Man Publius if we are to consider Mistra to have been the landing place.

Our next consideration is not merely whether they were capable of walking far, but how far it was necessary for them to walk.

At Wardija there is a church, built in 1616 on the site of earlier churches. This church bears the name San Pawl Milqi, which means 'Saint Paul welcomed'. A very old tradition associated this church with the villa of Publius. When Capt. Smith wrote his book in 1848 he did not have the advantage of the findings of modern archeology. In the 1960's the Italian Missione Archeologica excavated this site and revealed the remains of a large Roman villa built more than a hundred years before Paul landed on Malta. This villa is part of a group of buildings, but is nearest to the sea and faces Salina Bay. From it one can look across the Bur-marrad plain, beyond the creek (now salt-pans) across the bay to Qawra point. Associated with the villa are the remains of a flour mill and an olive-pippa for processing oil. There is also indication that there was some form of ceramics industry in operation. Clearly this was the centre of an estate.

Here then we have evidence of people who lived in the vicinity when Paul came and buildings which could be considered as the likely place for him to have been given shelter. The Italian Mission found other things. They found stone fragments which had engraved upon them a cross and a fish, which were early Christian symbols. They found a room which because of its separate entrances and exits seemed to have been a room of significance, which over a period seemed progressively to have become distinct from the other buildings. In other words it seems to have had a special function and it has been suggested that it became a Christian meeting place. Whether special significance can be placed upon the cistern in this room is not clear. Here then is a site which can rightly claim to be considered as the place where Publius "received us, and lodged us courteously three days" as the narrative puts it.

Assuming this to be the site where Paul had his first night's sleep in Malta; and no other site has ever been named or claimed, we return to the question of distances.

We have traced the ordeal of the travellers, through a devastating voyage, exhausted from lack of sleep, the trials of the relentless storm, the back-aching task of unloading a whole shipload of grain in a vessel swaying and tossing in mighty waves, summoning their last energy for a terrifying swim ashore and finally sitting soaked to the skin until their tired muscles were cramped. They would not be in a condition to walk far even if there was much daylight left. They certainly could not have walked from Mistra beach to Wardija. I have tried it when fit and it took a long time. I would not have been ready to attempt it if I had gone through what those men had experienced.

On the other hand from Qawra to Wardija would not have been so unreasonable!

Earlier we considered what the occupants of the ship saw at dawn which made them decide on their course of action. As the Weymouth translation puts it "their objective was, if possible to run the ship aground into this inlet". They thought the north east wind might take them there so they hoisted the sail (most translations indicate the foresail), let the anchors drop into the sea in approximately fifteen fathoms and loosed the bands that secured the rudder oars at the rear of the ship. That was their intention, but it did not work out as they had hoped. They had no knowledge of the currents in that part of the bay, they would not know how much rudder to use and they struck the reef and ran aground. The spot is described by the Greek words 'topon dithalasson' (where two seas meet). Capt. Smith thought that the islands of Selmunette answered this description. In a footnote, however, he explains that the best translation of the words is 'isthmus' which exactly describes Qawra point!

Dr. Burridge, referring to Qawra says that 'it could be held to satisfy the conditions of being a place where two seas meet'. He also says in the same paragraph 'it consists of low lying jagged rocks with the occasional underwater shelf. The rocks are low enough for the bather to take an ordinary dive and the underwater shelves enable him to land safely again. The water, save on the shelves, is everywhere deep'. He adds that it is a 'very nasty place in a gregale'. But then, what part of the coast is not?

Having examined the difficulties which prevent confident acceptance of the generally accepted site, let us now consider the merits of Salina Bay.

Referring to the map on page 18 it can be seen that we arrive at a fifteen fathom mark off Ghallis. An anchorage at this point answers all the conditions of the dawn perception of inlet, creek, bay, shore or sandy beach whichever translation one considers. With a north east wind blowing, the seamen would consider that they had a chance to get at least near to the shelter of the inlet, although well aware of the danger of the reef at Qawra and the possibility of rocks or sandbanks in the centre of the bay. A hundred yards or so nearer Qawra and they might have seen the buildings at Wardija, or those in the south eastern corner of the bay (see Salina Tombs section). That they did not, implies that the headland at Ghallis obscured this information. Except for the reef to the north and the underwater shelves to which Burridge has drawn attention, the water around Qawra is deep. This is an important point. It would enable the doomed ship to get comparatively close inshore before it ran aground, thus reducing the distance for the men to swim to safety. It also answers the condition arising from the soldiers fear, that the prisoners might be able to escape. The ship could, in fact, have stuck fast on the inner side of the isthmus.

In this setting the size of the ship is a helpful factor.

Being close to the shore its size would of itself make possible a small area of calmer water, sheltering the struggling victims from the wind.[1] Because of the position of the overnight anchorage it is probable that no islanders had as yet seen anything of the ship or the survivors. They, for their part, would have been too engrossed in the terrible things happening to them to be looking anywhere other than towards that part of the shore they were inevitably approaching. There are two possibilities as to what happened next. Either they would seek shelter from the gregale, by moving over to the other side of the headland (and thus be first seen by the natives in St. Paul's Bay and so lay the foundations for tradition); or they would seek to reach the creek which had been their original objective and ultimately discover habitations there, and beyond, the villa of Publius. On either route they would have found vegetation to provide twigs for a fire. We know that Salina Bay had inhabitants, (see later section) we can only guess, and it is a reasonable guess, that St. Paul's Bay had. In either case we have circumstances which make it reasonable to believe that it was physically possible to get to the Wardija villa of Publius on the day of the shipwreck.

The reason we know there were inhabitants in the south eastern corner of Salina Bay is the existence of tombs from the Roman period covering many generations and which are the subject of detailed consideration later in this book. The people living in this community would be the most likely to notice a ship aground at Qawra. They were probably the first hospitable Maltese that Paul met.

To test this theory I was not content merely to walk again and again all round these bays and to gingerly seek a footing on the jagged rocks at the extreme end of Qawra point. I thought it equally important to follow the supposed course of the ship itself. So it was that I chartered a boat for the special voyage asking the captain to follow as near as possible the fifteen fathom line. As the boat was about fifty feet long and with the deck about twelve feet above sea level, this seemed a fair comparison with a Roman ship as far as viewing the coastline was concerned. I warned the captain that I would want him to stop at short notice. I watched with interest as the Ghallis tower drew nearer noting the waves breaking over the Ghallis rocks. This could have been what the seamen had become aware of in the darkness of the night which had led the captain to take soudings. Qawra point was almost straight ahead, but slightly south and slowly the western side of Salina Bay began to appear. As soon as I caught the first glimpse of the salt pans I asked the captain to stop the ship. The south east corner of the bay was hidden. Only the highest point of the Salina Bay Hotel could be seen (and that is twentieth century); otherwise all the eastern side of the bay was obscured by Ghallis headland. From this spot it was not possible to see San Pawl Milqi or Salina habitations. If anchored at this spot Paul and his companions would have seen no buildings, only a bay and creek with sandy appearance. I asked the captain how deep the water was and he told me it was about fifteen fathoms.

I then asked the captain to continue, as long as it was safe to do so. We got suprisingly close to the inner side of the isthmus of Qawra, so close that without wrecking his ship to prove it I was satisfied that it was a swimmable distance. We made our way out to sea again at a safe distance beyond the Qawra reef and into St. Paul's Bay. Having seen Qawra, it seemed a mightly long swim to Mistra from the exposed rocks of Selmunette!

One of the many interesting people I have met in Malta was the experienced diver Tony Micallef-Borg. I had learned that in the course of diving he had found various Roman objects off the Maltese coast, so the next day I sought him out. "Tell me" I urged, "Where exactly did you find the part of a Roman anchor off Qawra?" He fetched the map and with great care worked out the spot. He pointed to a position remarkably close to the spot where I had first asked the captain to stop the ship! "At what depth?" I asked. "At about one hundred feet" was his reply.[2] Then he went on to tell me of pieces of Roman pottery which had been found off the inner curve of Qawra. In other words, in the area where I had estimated Paul's ship to have been wrecked! He explained that storms sometimes disturbed the sand and so revealed hidden amphorae.

Before coming to my next discovery I want to draw attention to one or two points of detail.

We have already noted that the sailors sought to thrust the

ship to the beach or shore which they had seen in the early light. They did not in fact succeed in their intention. They struck elsewhere. The narrative makes this clear. Thus, in looking for the landing place we do not have to look for a beach or inlet. They did not reach that part of the shore.

A French map of 1677 which refers to the shipwreck, indicates, in error, the Salines Nouvelle (new salt pans) at the extreme inner reaches of St. Paul's Bay instead of Salina Bay. Thus, if not associating the shipwreck with the bay where the salt pans are, at least it demonstrates a measure of uncertainty regarding the traditional area of the shipwreck. Other maps, some of which might be copies of earlier ones could perpetuate an error based on vague information.

Today there is a square tower at Qawra similar to others round the island. A Venetian map of 1689 shows a round tower at Qawra. A French map of 1717 shows the tower at Kaura (Qawra) to be round as distinct from the square one marked at Ghallis on the same map. In several places in Malta the remains of round towers are still to be seen. They are from the Roman era.

In 1975 I went to Italy, partly to discuss the Salina Bay catacombs with leading archaeologists, also because I wanted to examine and photograph a fourth century ivory diptych at the Bargello museum, in Florence. This has three scenes of St. Paul in Malta. I was most interested in the shipwreck episode carved upon it. Later, visiting S. Paolo fuori le Mura in Rome, I was struck by an oil painting of the shipwreck scene. I was particularly impressed by the fact that although the ivory carving naturally clothed the figures in the flowing garments of Roman days (when it was carved) and the oil painting displayed mediaeval dress, (the period when painted), the stance of Paul himself was remarkably similar, the turn of the head, the line of the shoulders, the angle of the feet, the arm bent from the elbow with snake dangling from the hand over a blazing fire. There are a hundred ways in which this episode could have been depicted, but here was a similar pose of the central figure. On enquiry, I learned that the painting was a copy. It had been painted in the fourteenth century.

Now when an artist sets out to convey an incident from a narrative, he has the choice of depending entirely upon his imagination, or by trying to reconstruct from facts supplied, or from models or landscapes before him. Whether the ivory carving was a source of inspiration is merely a matter of conjecture, but the oil painting itself contains some very interesting detail. People are clambouring out of the sea onto rocks (not sand as at Mistra). The sea from which they are emerging is in the foreground. The land slopes upwards towards the left of the picture and there is open sea beyond demonstrating that this is a promontory and at the left hand side of a bay. Help is coming over the hill from figures obviously representing the natives and there at the crown of the slope is a round tower. In the fourteenth century there was a round tower at Qawra point on the spot where the square tower now stands! The background gives further interesting information. You do not see a skyline like this whatever direction you look in St. Paul's Bay. Examine the hill to the left of the picture. Anyone standing in Salina Bay near the salt pans and looking towards San Pawl Milqi will recognise that flat-topped hill. It is unmistakeably il Qolla. It is clear that the artist associates Qawra with San Paul Milqi. He is trying to tell the whole story of the landing, the hospitality, the snake-bite and the reception by Publius in one picture. To do so he has had to transfer the villa and other buildings to the only spot available on the canvas. Despite the recent addition of tons of additional debris for building purposes at Qawra point one can note the similarities in slope between the old painting and the modern photographs. The evidence for Qawra as the place of landing is very strong.

Before moving on to the next stage of our study of Paul in Malta I want to draw attention to one other thing. Dunstan Ballanti has pointed out that Latin has not survived the later cultures and hardly any words remain that show their Latin origin. As one by one all the things we have considered above, presented themselves to my mind, I was intrigued by this comment. In looking at the old maps of the middle ages a factor struck me quite forcibly. Salina Bay did not bear this name until the salt pans were made in the days of the Knights. Before that, the bay was identified by various versions of a similar name. The variations were adaptions according to the nationality of the map maker grappling with an unusual language, thus in different centuries we have Benhouarrat, Benhonorate, Benorrat, Benorat, but the one that caught my eye was Benniarrad. Could it be that this is a corruption, through all the language changes of the island, of the Latin Bene ara (kindly refuge) – for this is exactly what Salina Bay would have seemed to those weary survivors?

If there are still any who favour the theory put forward by Capt. Smith, I invite them to choose a winter's day and a party of 276 volunteers, some of them non-swimmers and at least one who is sixty years of age and set them off from Selmunette for the afternoon swim! Unaided, the whole party must get safely ashore. If, after that, about twenty of them, including the sixty year old, can walk to San Pawl Milqi before dark, the conditions of the narrative will have been met (other than the fasting and the cargo unloading). Meanwhile, my party based off Qawra point would have time for a long rest at Bugibba and would be waiting at San Pawl Milqi to welcome the brave traditionalists!

To many it may seem of little consequence which of two adjoining bays was the right one. The important point is that Salina Bay completely authenticates the New Testament story and draws attention to the special significance of the catacombs at Salina Bay. Were people buried there who met Paul?

left: 14th century oil painting

above: skyline – il Qolla from Salina

D. Whitehouse

above: Qawra. slope and tower. *below: Qawra, inner curve of bay.*

above: jagged rocks at Qawra point.   below: Qawra, where two seas meet

Roman villa of Publius

Roman villa of Publius with olive pippa for pulping olives.

Roman villa of Publius looking towards Naxxar

Public toilets. Roman baths. Ghajn Tuffieha

Like a crack across the island.

Salina: ancient cart ruts.

Salina. water container at roadside adjacent to ancient well

ancient road across Bur-marrad.

THE CHIEF MAN

We now move on to an investigation of the Malta Paul found, what happened while he was there and the effect of his visit on subsequent history. To do this we need to consider what sort of people the inhabitants of the islands were and what impact the Roman Empire had upon them.

People far more qualified than I, have written illuminating books of the earlier ages. It is sufficient for our purpose to note that Melita, as it was known in Roman times, was formerly a Phoenician colony and that Aramaic was probably still spoken by the natives. This was a language Paul was able to speak, so that he at least of the survivors would have been able to converse with the local folk.

Luke, the writer, draws attention to the hospitality of the Chief Man, Publius. Our usual experience is to find that prominent members of a community are somewhat selective about whom they invite to their homes. The action of Publius is at once striking. We can understand red-carpet treatment for a visitor of standing whose coming had been anticipated, but the sudden arrival of a motley collection of foreign refugees is another matter. No doubt Julius wore some badge of office. As a centurion of the Augustan band he certainly commanded considerable respect anywhere in the Roman world. After all, he was on the Emperor's business. His was a special assignment. Priority treatment must be given him. Because of his status it is probable that when, at Myra, Julius had said that he wanted passage to Rome for his prisoners and their guard, the ship authorities had no option but to agree. Perhaps that had been an added reason for the captain making the unwise decision to put to sea so late in the sailing season. We can appreciate that when the news reached Publius of how important a visitor had suddenly come ashore there was much to do to get quarters ready, but for the chief man of the island to have to accommodate prisoners of Caesar as well was an unexpected development! The elite of the Special Branch was one thing, but prisoners, some of whom might be mere fodder for some arena spectacle was another.

Not only did Publius welcome Paul and his companions to his estate, and, it would seem, to his own dwelling, but he personally introduced them to his own family, which is truly remarkable when one considers the rank of the host and the status of an imperial prisoner. It is so remarkable that it draws attention to the character of this man.

Luke does not state that the whole company of 276 were entertained on the estate of Publius although when we visualise the probable boundaries this could well have been likely. Luke certainly uses the expression 'entertained us hospitably' so at least Paul's friends were included. To have split the prisoners into groups for billetting would have meant splitting the guard also, which might have been considered inadvisable. Temporary accommodation for the remainder might well have been found closer to the scene of the shipwreck. As there was a settlement at the mouth of the creek, which from now on I shall refer to by the ancient name of Beniarrad, this could well be where shelter was provided for some. An unexpected party of 276 guests was no small problem!

Tradition claims that the chapel at Wardija marks the site where Paul first slept in Malta. As mentioned already archaeology has proved the existence of a Roman villa of the appropriate date at this spot. Here, it seems probable, Paul and his weary companions were warmly welcomed and here the first conversations between Paul and Publius took place.

It would not be long before the story of Paul and the snake was common knowledge in the Publius household, probably first learned from the servants. There are no poisonous snakes in Malta today, but this is no argument for saying that there were none in AD 60. Maltese museums demonstrate that there were many animals and reptiles once living in the island which are now extinct. Luke is hardly likely to have given space to the episode if it did not happen. It was an incident vividly remembered by the inhabitants who were present. The nature of their incredulous reaction is typical of the generation steeped in superstition. That this influenced Publius in his decision to offer hospitality is unlikely. It would, however, have assured a respectful approach and his father's illness was obviously on his mind.

One of the first things that Publius would want to know was what Paul had done to become an imperial prisoner. That Paul was both a Roman citizen and a Jew would make him an intriguing visitor. On both counts an administrator would have to be cautious in his treatment because the status of both ensured privileges. Julius would make it clear that Procurator Porcius Festus had been reluctant to send Paul to Rome and that he would not have done so had not the prisoner exercised his rights as a Roman citizen to appeal to Caesar. What perhaps was not appreciated by Julius was that if Paul had not appealed to Caesar, the alternative would have been a trial at Jerusalem where his chances of survival were slim. Publius would want to know more about the nature of this man's faith which could have taken him to such lengths. It was almost unusual visitor who had come to Malta.

Paul could scarcely have hoped for a better start. His fellow-travellers could testify to the fact that if they had listened to him in the first place there would have been no shipwreck. They would testify to his qualities of leadership which had brought decisiveness in the near panic situation the night before. His had been the calm influence persuading everyone to eat and prepare themselves for the ordeal ahead. It was he who had sat calmly in the storm, breaking bread in such an awe-inspiring fashion as to be like a communion meal with the Christ whom he served. His impact upon the natives sitting around the fire was so impressive that they had mentally raised him to the status of a god. The man whose mark of identification was a manacle and whose presence justified a squad of special soldiers, had become the man of the hour even before he had been honoured by the hospitality of the chief man of the island.

It has been assumed that Publius was a Roman, but this was not necessarily the case. In minor regions of administration authority was often vested in local chieftains who became responsible to the Provincial authority of which it was part. Melita was presumably controlled from Sicily.

The reference to the 'estate' has very much a rural ring about it. It does not suggest an official palace or seat of power that we would normally associate with a governing official. The farming and commercial association with the villa at Wardija, revealed by the archeologists, suggests a private enterprise rather than a court. In the fourteenth century, a priest wrote that he had seen an indent passing down from father to son Publius the lands at Burmarrad. Other writers have referred to the 'heirs plot'. A punic inscription found on the site which reads, 'Banay son of Himilk son of . . . . ' and thought to have been imported from elsewhere could nevertheless have been part of a record of succession, especially if Publius had punic rather than Roman ancestry. Archeologists have also indicated that the villa revealed a leaning towards a punic life-style, which encouraged the conclusion that Publius was probably Maltese.

We know, of course, that it was customary for Roman soldiers on retirement to be given land on the fringes of the empire and status to go with it as a means of keeping minor regions in order but in the case of Publius we have no evidence that he had been a soldier and we are dealing with a situation where both father and son are firm residents. The son was the most important man on the island. There is no indication that the father held office at all. Publius would appear to have been selected on merit. The office does not appear to be hereditary as the father was still alive. A similar circumstance is perhaps illustrated by the inscription found in Gozo which names both a father and son being honoured at a time when the younger was the more significant.[3]

Whether Publius was of Maltese or Roman ancestry, whether Wardija was his chief residence or whether he spent much of his time at a seat of administration at Rabat we cannot tell. The one thing we know for certain is that the first three days of Paul's stay in Malta was at the hospitality of the Chief Man.

The effect on Publius is one of the remarkable results of Paul's shipwreck on Malta. Not only is it claimed that he became a convert, but tradition has it that he became a leader of the Church. The fact that he was Chief Man of the island with administrative responsibility would immediately have created problems for him. There would be a conflict of loyalty to Caesar and his indebtedness to Paul and his adherence to the new Christian faith. It was the sort of conflict which was soon to reach a point of crisis for Christians throughout the Roman world. As a convert he would certainly give the fullest facility for Paul to preach his gospel.

Later Malta became a municipium. The transition may have marked the end of an era of Maltese freedom of administration, possibly hastened because of subsequent laxity in containing the Christian development begun under the sympathetic control of Publius.

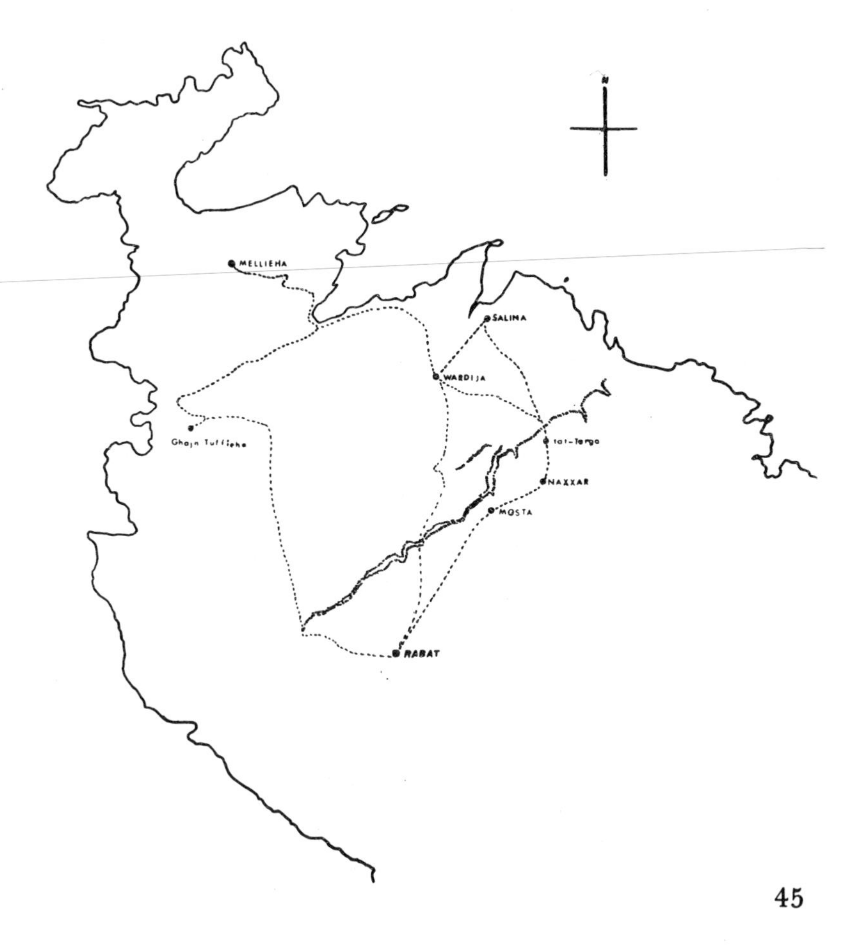

WHERE PAUL VISITED

Reference has been made earlier to the settlement at the mouth of the creek in what is now Salina Bay. We now investigate this part of the Bur-marrad estate.

On the east side of the bay about a hundred yards south of the Salina Bay Hotel and opposite the salt-pans, a road branches inland from the coast road. In less than another hundred yards one sees on the left the Annunciate chapel which old maps confirm has been in existence for several hundred years and probably, like San Pawl Milqi, was the site of earlier churches. The road at this point turns right towards Naxxar and two secondary roads create a crossroads. Roughly parallel to the Naxxar road pointing to the chapel and on the right hand side as you face it, can be seen among the uneven rocks examples of the famous 'cart-ruts' cut into the solid rock. These cart-ruts are to be found in many parts of the island. That they are pre-Roman has been conclusively proved. They are memorials to the days before wheeled vehicles and were obviously to facilitate the transport of loads over uneven rocky territory. Another clear set just below the village of Naxxar points in the direction of Salina Bay. So these near the Annunciata chapel are perhaps the continuation of this ancient route. An interesting hour can be spent tracing them beyond the chapel and along the lower slopes of the hill towards the bay. You find that they lead through the grounds of the Salina Bay Hotel near the fougasse and down to the shore of the bay itself.[4]

This is of importance to our study, because it is obvious that from early times this route to the sea from higher parts inland implies that this bay has had a significance as a trading point over a long period. That these cart-ruts were still being used in the first century AD has been stated by other writers. That Romans used the bay is known from the anchors and pottery found in it. The implication is that some sort of port must have existed here. For a port to function it must have inhabitants in the vicinity. That there were habitations is confirmed by the fact that from all over this hill, that leads down to the east shore and the salt-pans, farmers have discovered Roman pottery and glassware. At one point on the hillside not far from the chapel is what could be a filled-in Roman well. The presence of inhabitants at Beniarrad in Roman times is therefore established. That occupation was continuous would seem likely as long as the need for trading existed. This was unlikely to have continued after the Arab invasion of 870 AD when trading with Sicily and Italy would ultimately cease. It probably came to an end earlier with the split empire and increasing Byzantine influence in Malta.

The next information we have which confirms the existence of a settlement in this area is to be found in the Salina Bay catacombs. The conspicuous ones lie a little further up the hill from the Annunciata chapel, but in fact the area over which the tombs are scattered stretch from a point above the cart-ruts by the crossroads right across the lower parts of the hill to a point quite close to the drive entrance of the Salina Bay Hotel. For the patient searcher there is evidence to be found of the foundation of buildings. Because I believe the Salina Bay catacombs to be important to our study a special section has been reserved for it later.

It has been stated by more than one writer that Salina Bay in Roman times stretched inland as far as Wardija. This I doubt, although it is probable that the creek itself did with marshy ground on its eastern side where the ground is lower. This would justify the belief that small craft may have worked up and down this useful strip of water. By the very formation of the land, however, strangers on a ship anchored beyond the Ghallis headland would not have been aware of this.

Knowing that in winter, parts of Bur-marrad would be marshy, the question of communications between the administrative centre of the estate at Wardija and the Beniarrad settlement has to be considered. The Italian Archeological

Mission report mentions that industry at the villa included the production of olive oil, flour and even ceramics. If any export was involved Beniarrad was the obvious place for it to be loaded on visiting ships. To stand in the middle of Bur-marrad one notes the curious fact that the Annunciata chapel and that at San Pawl Milqi quite clearly face each other. Crossing the fields of Bur-marrad is a straight stone-surfaced road with broad walled sides, which one imagines could have linked the two places before the modern road to Naxxar broke its line. This could well have been the ancient route across the marsh.[5]

If some of the shipwreck survivors had to be billetted at Beniarrad or Bugibba, contact between members of the split group of travellers would have been both necessary and inevitable. Unless Paul was denied movement it would not be at all surprising for him to visit Beniarrad to examine the scene of the shipwreck. Weeks before, when the ship had docked at Sidon Julius had permitted Paul to visit friends. It is unlikely that he would have denied a similar facility in Malta.

It is where Paul went to after the three days at the villa which we must now consider.

Through the centuries, stories have been passed on claiming that Paul had been connected with a particular spot other than San Pawl Milqi. The most famous is the grotto beneath the parish church of St. Paul's beyond the walls, Rabat, where it is claimed that Paul was imprisoned. There are a number of other claims, some of which have encouraged scornful comment over the years. Unless we take the view that Paul spent the entire three months in one place, we have to admit that theoretically he could have visited any part of the island. Ultimately the Roman Catholic Church recognised Publius as a saint because of his deeds in the years after his conversion. Remembering this, one finds it difficult to believe that such a man would have confined Paul to such a miserable grotto as that at Rabat. Nevertheless, the tradition is so old and evidence of previous churches on the spot so early, and because it is in an area of the old Roman town, one can confidently subscribe to the view that Paul spent time in that vicinity and probably close to that spot.

It is many years now since Dunstan Ballanti wrote at great length to point out that no evidence whatever has been found to support any claim that the Cathedral church at Mdina was built over the original site of the palace of Publius, adding 'until the Arabs came in 870AD the site over which Mdina stands was practically a desert.' He further points out that pilgrims to the Holy Land, halting at Malta in the course of their journeyings, ignored the Cathedral church, but inevitably visited St. Paul's grotto. Roman remains have, in fact, been found at Mdina but do not seem to have been connected either with Publius or Christianity.[6] Although the St. Paul's grotto at Rabat does not impress as a reasonable habitation to be provided by the friendly Publius, the fact that there may have been a church here as early as 100AD, according to Ballanti, does not seem unreasonable. This spot, St. Paul's Beyond the Walls, is on the edge of the original Roman town of Melita. It will be recalled that on the morning of the shipwreck, the concern of the soldiers that the prisoners might escape had prompted them to suggest that they be killed. Now that Paul was becoming increasingly popular, they may have been equally officious and may have felt that town confinement could be more effective than the rural setting of Wardija. If there was a prison on the island this is where it would be. Bellanti contends that St. Paul's beyond the Walls was the only church in Malta for many centuries. This depends, of course, on what constitutes a church, a matter which will be discussed later.

Another spot which claims association with the visit of Paul is at Mellieha, a village several miles west of the villa and across hilly country. The name is Pheonician in origin and means 'salty' from the ancient salt-pans in its bay which were there in Roman days. Set on two hills, the cliff faces are honeycombed with caves which for thousands of years have been used as habitations. Some still are used as residences. In one of the caves the goddess Calypso was said to have lived before her departure 'unto the bosom of the gods'. This was therefore a sacred cave in ancient times. It is claimed that this cave became the first Christian church in Mellieha, that a painting by Luke of the Virgin Mary was to be seen there and that bishops on their way to the Council of Milevium in Africa in 409AD stopped at Melliaha and reconsecrated the sanctuary.

That the cave of Calypso could have become a Christian

church is not unlikely, inasmuch as Christians took over many temples in the course of time and used them as places of worship. It is not unreasonable to believe that Paul or one of his companions founded a church here. The question of a painting by Luke is harder to accept. With Paul, and presumably Luke also, as a doctor and co-evangelist, so busy receiving people from all over the island throughout the three months stay, the latter would not have had time for painting pictures. It is unlikely that artists' materials were readily available at the Roman equivalent of the general store. As an artist myself, as late as 1978, I could not find the colours I wanted in a shopping centre as large as Sleima and had to search in Valletta before meeting with success. Up in the hills above the ancient town of Ephesus in Turkey there is a shrine where it is claimed that miraculous cures have taken place. Closeby is said to be the spot where Mary, the Mother of Jesus, resided in her old age, having been taken to Ephesus by the Apostle John at the dying wish of Christ on the Cross. If Luke ever met her it was more likely to have been here than anywhere else. As he wrote his Gospel and the Acts of the Apostles late in the century he must have been still a comparatively young man when he came to Malta in AD 60. The picture at Mellieha is of a teenage girl. In 60 AD the Mother of Jesus must have been at least 75 years of age! Another difficulty that we have in connection with this painting is that the worship of the Blessed Virgin Mary was not part of the teaching of the church in the first century AD. The first known painting of the Blessed Virgin Mary was mid-second century and found in St. Priscilla in Rome. It would seem that this painting must be classified as a work of imagination probably painted in the fourth century AD.[7]

The other claims of association take us to the eastern end of the Bur-marrad plain to Naxxar and San Pawl tat-Targa. The former because it claimed to be the first in the faith and the latter, which means 'St. Paul of the staircase or steps' because that was the route he took.

The geography is interesting. The flat low-lying fields of Bur-marrad suddenly meet a high inland cliff-face, the line of which continues in both directions like a crack across the island, presumably the result of the catastrophic earthquake thousands of years ago which lead to much of the island's civilization disappearing under the sea. It is later than the cart-ruts which disappear into the sea in places. The remnants of this civilisation are to be found off shore around the coast at depths as much as the height of this inland cliff. No doubt as marine archaeologists will yet prove this adds to the claims of Malta to be the ancient Atlantis.

Today modern roads approach this geographical hurdle at two points using hairpin bends to reach the higher level. In Paul's day the climb would have been extremely difficult. Hence tat-Targa, the staircase, is an apt description because rock-steps would probably have been necessary to reach the clifftop. Paul would not have used this more difficult route unless he was indeed visiting the region of Naxxar as it is not on the direct route to Rabat. The old tradition is that inhabitants of Naxxar were the first to embrace the Christian faith when Paul passed through it on his way to Rabat for the first time, hence the parish motto 'Prior crediti' – 'the first-born of the faith'. In view of the winter floods and the steepness of the climb it is unlikely that this route would have been chosen when journeying from Wardija to Rabat, unless there was some special reason.

I agree with Bellanti when he says that 'Paul's first converts seem to have been nearer the shipwreck', in other words, in the Salina Bay area; but evangelicals of any Christian denomination will declare that the first contacts are not necessarily the first converts. From the information provided in the Acts of the Apostles the first convert in all probability was the father of Publius. He may have been living somewhere other than in the Wardija villa for Luke specifically states that Paul 'visited' him. This could explain the origin of 'first in the faith' being applied to Naxxar. We assume the whole of the Bur-marrad plain to be the family estate in view of the record of the fourteenth century indent. With tat-Targa on its perimeter.

Luke does not state that the sick father was living or even staying at the villa of Publius. The process of visiting implies a journey. It is not unreasonable to deduce that there was a dwelling or dwellings at Naxxar. The route of the cart-ruts indicates links between places of habitation. If at the time of the illness, the father of Publius had been within the Wardija villa complex adjoining the marshy area, it would not be surprising if Paul and Dr. Luke advised removal to higher ground. Here Bellanti's theory that the derivation of the name Naxxar is an active noun from the verb tonxor (to dry) has some point. This higher land would be a healthier region than the marsh area.

This leads to an interesting thought concerning Bellanti's suggested derivation of Mosta as being from the Maltese adjective 'fostani' meaning 'between first and third' and 'wostani' meaning 'middle'. If Paul visited Naxxar on the way to Rabat the next or 'middle' place on the route would be Mosta. Few places are listed on surviving documents so it cannot be proved except by archaeologists, if there were dwellings there in those days. Extracts from a letter of 1623 mention a village which 'faced seawards on the slopes overlooking Weid-il-Ghasel'.

On the crowded deck during the weeks of the voyage from Caesarea, Paul would have made friends among his fellow travellers. If some of them had been housed on part of the estate other than at Wardija, and in all probability at Beniarrad, it would not be unreasonable for him to ask permission to visit them on the way to Rabat. Flooding of the plain may have made a roundabout route via Beniarrad more practicable anyhow, perhaps ferrying across the mouth of the creek and following the higher ground north of the plain.

Wherever the sick father was housed, the fact that Paul visited him reveals an element of freedom. We note that he was not 'taken'. Whether, after the visit, he returned to one of the buildings associated with the villa, as is suggested by the significant room described by the Italian Archaeological Mission, or whether he was confined at Rabat, or both, is not clear. Wherever he settled down, his reputation grew rapidly and people from all over the island travelled to see him, seeking his help. So the next thing we are sure of was his accessibility.

The Maltese aristocracy may have been confined to a few families which makes all the more intriguing the effect the conversion of the Chief Man, Publius, would have had. The conversion of a few fishermen, peasants and slaves would have caused little stir. The conversion of the Chief Man would have been sensational and probably progressive in its effects in a community cut off from the influences of mainland culture for much of the year. If the common people were granted easy access to the prisoner, as seems clear from Luke's account, than those of higher status would no doubt be able to arrange for Paul to be brought to them. That Paul was accustomed to fraternising with the higher eschelons of society is known from his dealings with the City Treasurer at Corinth and from the high esteem in which he was held by the Asiarchs in Ephesus. Indeed, during the Caesarean imprisonment a meeting with a king had taken place. Paul could find his level in any company and 'being all things to all men' was an aspect of this capacity. It is for this reason that we should not rule out the possibility that Paul travelled widely in the island.

BACKGROUND

For the Maltese people the winter of 60 AD was an unusual one. When once the shipwreck had ceased to be a nine days wonder and the last fragments of wreckage had been collected from the beach to be made into furniture, or mend huts, or add to fuel stocks, the daily routine still had to be pursued on the farm and in the craftsmen's shops. The influx of nearly three hundred strangers most of whom spoke only Greek or Latin was a bit of an administrative problem! As the corn ship had probably been commandeered for the voyage in the name of Caesar there was probably some obligation for authority to care for the survivors. Publius would have to get his officials to organise shelter and provisions and clothing. So large a group of refugees idle for three months could be an administrative headache. There would be complaints to sort out – stories of unfair treatment, goods stolen, women molested. The seamen and freelance passengers would probably be more of a problem that the prisoners who could be more easily disciplined and regimented. As in every generation there would be the more adventurous who would set off on sight-seeing tours. The crew of the Castor & Pollox were also roaming the island looking for something to do. Their shore leave might well have been upsetting the local inhabitants. All the visitors were bound for Italy and most were looking forward to the excitements of life in the great city of the Emperor. Rural Malta would seem a bit dull so they would aim for Rabat and that was probably where Paul, the preaching prisoner was located.

We might wonder what sort of accommodation Paul would

be given during his stay. Although many of the inhabitants were housed in simple huts and cave dwellings, we know from the excavated Roman villa at Rabat and the baths of Ghajn Tuffieha and elsewhere that Roman residents at least had more luxurious living quarters. The work of the Museum Department of Malta over the years has produced considerable evidence of Roman occupation in and near Rabat, which enables us to picture a well organised town at the centre of the island.

Rabat was the place to which people from elsewhere in the island would most frequently travel for business transactions of all kinds. It was here that the special events would no doubt take place. Marble that once adorned the buildings and other treasures have long since been taken from the island by Napoleon and other invaders, but sufficient fragments remain for us to know that opulence existed alongside poverty. The remains of Roman culture in the island is now so sparse, however, that we have to look at contemporary architecture elsewhere to build up a picture.

Fortunately we have vivid examples of the lifestyle of this very generation where the dating is absolutely beyond doubt. When the volcano Vesuvius erupted in 79AD it buried Pompeii and Herculaneum in volcanic ash and mud and thereby preserved much of the property in the exact state as when the people in them died. Thanks to the patient work of archaeologists we are able to see houses, rooms and furniture exactly as they were on that tragic August day. When Paul eventually left Malta for Rome he was to pass quite close to these doomed towns, for he disembarked at Puteoli in the Bay of Naples and could not have failed to see Vesuvius dominating the skyline. He would have seen across the bay the magnificance of Herculaneum sweeping down to the shoreline and in the background a glimpse of Pompeii.

From these remarkably preserved towns we can actually see how the Romans lived in Paul's day. We can see the types of wall decoration, the nature of their bakeries and roadside shops, the craftsmen's tools and places where they worked and a thousand details of domestic and commercial life. We know a lot about their tableware and storage vessels, the eating implements and glassware used. We know that engineering had reached an advanced stage with the use of pumps and water-valves. We even have information down to such things as medicines and recipes. For instance for festival cake 'Pound thoroughly in a mortar two pounds of cheese; when this is done add one pound of wheat flour; add an egg, and knead the whole thoroughly. Pat it into shape, place it on leaves, and bake slowly on the hearth under an earthenware cover'. The honey recipes would probably have been popular in Malta which was famous for its bees. The remains of Roman beehives still exist in Malta.

Because of his Jewish background, Paul would probably be influenced by the strict eating laws of the Jews and would refrain from certain dishes.

Although he was accounted a scholar, Paul did not belong to the leisured classes. He was a craftsman accustomed to working with his hands. His hometown Tarsus in Cilicia, (now southern Turkey) was famous for its cilicium cloth woven from goats' hair, from which waterproof coverings were made. From time to time we know that he worked at this trade to earn his keep and was, in fact, described as a tent-maker. Presumably in Melita the occasion to work at his trade would not arise, although the island had also been famous for the best known sailcloth of the day. This would no doubt interest him much and provide a link with local craftsmen. Judging by the popularity Paul achieved from the very beginning it is not improbable that at some stage he was taken to see some of the island crafts, which he, as a practical man would understand.

Whether he would be provided with a proper wooden bed as found in middle class homes of the generation is doubtful, but wool mattresses were common and probably available in Melita.

Paul was essentially interested in meeting people and telling them of the spiritual power which had transformed his life from a persecutor of Christians to an ambassador for the faith he had persecuted. People would travel across the island to him and the fact that he could converse in Aramaic would be a great asset.

There is a tradition that Paul's parents came from a Pharisaic family who lived near lake Genassaret in northern Galilee and that they became wealthy Roman citizens when they moved to Tarsus in Cilicia. At all stages of his life religion seemed paramount. Power politics appeared not to matter to him. His whole life was spent waiting for the hand of God to show itself. During the years spent persecuting the Christians he believed he was fulfilling the will of God inasmuch as the Christians were deviants, followers of a blasphemer and rebels against the authority of the Law.

The revolutionary thing that had happened to him at conversion was that his religion took on a new dimension. The Jewish Law, which had been his whole life, had been fulfilled in Jesus. Because he had satisfied himself that Jesus was the Messiah long awaited by the Jews it was inevitable that he should also believe that they had reached the end of the age. As Jesus had manifested himself to him on the Damascus road,[8] so the day would soon come for his glorious return when only those who had made themselves ready would be able to share in the new age. Because the Gospel of Jesus was a gospel of love he must forever search, forever plead, forever reach out to gather in yet more converts before the 'Day of the Lord' came. For this reason he would gladly suffer shipwreck and hunger and bonds and lashes.

It was determination which took him from Tarsus to study at Jerusalem and led him into fanatical persecution and later drove him into missionary pioneering. He must always get beyond the next hill. In Perga he must see Attalia.[9] When there he looks up at the Mountains and is not content unless he can get beyond them to take his message into the interior. Every town was a stepping stone to the next. Time is previous, he must hurry on.

His singleminded persistence makes him not the best sort of person with whom to reason. He will soon make enemies. He will be misunderstood by people who mistake his characteristics for other things. He will be in disagreement with friends and companions and if they do not accept his judgement he will wash his hands of them. Mark becomes a casualty,[10] but, we may be sure, a casualty always burdening the evangelists' heart. His decision made, he cannot go back. The heartache he carries over many a weary mile. Many a time after he would feel that Mark would have been the ideal companion to have had at a point of testing.

There is no evidence that Paul ever married although this would have been expected of a Jew. If he ever had been married the nomadic existence of his evangelistic tours prevented him from having a normal home life. Even the apocryphal story of his association with Thekla is devoid of sexual content. He seemed to be a singleminded man who had little time for the satisfactions of the flesh. A wicked world seemed to be coming to an end and he sought to save as many as possible for the age to come. God had clearly brought him by storm to Melita so he must devote all his energies to bringing the Gospel to this island people.

Physically unattractive to the point of self-comment he nevertheless possessed a personality which commanded loyalty and more often than not, affection also. Timothy, left in charge at Ephesus, was moved to tears when they said good-bye at Miletus. That he sometimes annoyed people and attracted criticism there is little doubt as is clear from his attempts in his letters to correct certain misunderstandings about things he had said or done. If he had earned the respect of Julius the centurion and Publius the island chief, he could, on the other hand, have aroused resentment from some of the crew for being too ready with his advice and for implying, rightly or wrongly, that they had planned to desert a sinking ship. Some may have been won over in the light of subsequent events but others may have remained sullen and bitter for a long time and shown it during the winter months on the island.

His humility and diplomacy is exemplified in his ready willingness on arrival in Jerusalem, over two years before,[11] to accept a vow to quieten his critics within the Jerusalem church. His sensitivity over the obvious division between Gentile and Jewish Christians is seen in his untiring efforts to raise funds to help the impoverished Jewish brethren and he gets Gentiles to see to it! That this act of generosity should culminate in his arrest, while demonstrating this brotherly gesture, must have been both bewildering and saddening as for two long years he lay confined in the Caesarea jail, particularly as thereafter we hear of no efforts on his behalf from the Jerusalem leaders he had been trying to please.

He had been warned by many of the risks he was taking and the plots that were being hatched. He had taken the risks because he thought that his gesture would bind the church together. He had gone to Jerusalem bearing gifts from Gentile churches. The bearers of the gifts he had brought with him were Gentile converts, so that all might see what fine men were these new Christians. He had been arrested on the accusation of taking one of them into a forbidden part of the Temple, which he, as an ardent Jew would never have done. The seriousness of the offence is confirmed by archaeology for in 1871 and again in 1935 inscribed tablets were found, obviously from the wall which divided the inner area of the Temple which read 'Let no gentile enter within the balustrade and enclosure about the holy place; and whosoever is caught shall be responsible to himself because death follows'.

Imprisonment for so restless a character as Paul must have been a terrible frustration. There was so much to do and so little time left. The months of confinement must have been months of heartache. Because of this the very activity involved in a voyage to Rome must have been wonderfully refreshing to such an apostle. The kindly refuge of Melita must have been a benediction to a weary warrior and a time of spiritual rejuvenation preparing him for even more difficult days ahead in Rome. That he was provided with circumstances which enabled him to get on with the work to which he felt called, was a wonderful occurrence for one who knew that he was near the end of his career. That he had trustworthy companions to share the tasks must have been of inestimable value.

In these days when a court case is reported and we hear that the accused has been sentenced to five years imprisonment we get the impression that a fairly serious crime must have been committed. Most people overlook the fact that from the time Paul was arrested in Jerusalem to the end of his trial in Rome, he was never again a free man and if his trial ended in his death, which seems probable, then during the last five years of his life he was continuously a prisoner.

When he reached Malta, he had already been a prisoner for about two and a half years and was probably well over sixty years of age. However physically vigorous he may still have been, however mentally alert and certainly spiritually serene, nevertheless, his sufferings over many years had been so exacting that inevitably there must have been occasions of weariness and endless disappointment at the behaviour of lesser men, both friends and enemies. That he had enemies is a fact of history. That was why he was now a prisoner, and because of Jewish Law which he had once fanatically upheld.

The Malta that he came to may have provided him with a new type of missionary situation and an opportunity unlike any presented to him before in all his years of campaigning.

Enemies have been mentioned. When we study the missionary enterprises which Paul had been engaged in over the years and when we read the letters he wrote, the great stumblingblock throughout seems to have been the enemies either from the Jewish religion or from certain Jewish traditionalists within the Christian Church. They may have been very sincere and devout people, but they continually obstructed Paul's work by an insistence that all converts should abide by the fundamental ritual laws of Judaism. Paul stood his ground by pointing out that the Law had been superseded by Christ. In most countries around the Mediterranean, the Jewish religion was well established and recognised by Roman authority which even gave special privileges to Jews. The privileges began with Julius Caesar who had rewarded Jews who had soldiered with him. His gratitude led to protective laws which declared that the Jews should not be hindered by anybody from carrying out their sacrifices and other religious duties. Nobody should compel them to break their Sabbath, even when on military service, and they could be exempt from conscription to the army. There were many other conspicuous advantages which naturally caused envy in many places.

In major cities they had their own senate, headed by an ethnarch who had considerable public standing, they were permitted their own courts which could exact fines and even inflict scourging. We can therefore understand how it had come about, that Paul had been the object of special attention on a number of occasions and that, irrespective of whether Paul was quilty or not, the Jews had the right to raise questions concerning the breach of their religious laws.

This is not the place to discuss theological and other issues at stake which were at the root of Jewish opposition to Paul. Sufficient to point out that wherever he went, Paul seemed to commence his activity in the synagogue and sooner or later the opposition to what he was preaching developed and as a 'marked man' he became harrassed wherever he went.

In Malta it would, for the first time, be a situation in which there were no agitators to undermine his work. His opponents did not even know he was in Malta. They thought he was in Rome where there was a strong Jewish colony. The shipping routes were closed for the winter so they could not follow him. So, unhindered at last, Paul, the prisoner, was to have three months freed from obstructionists. Perhaps that is why Malta ever since has had such deeply religious people. One significant fact is that the last Christian Church which we know for certain to have been founded by Paul was in Malta.

From the beginning of the journey, we have noted that Julius had allowed Paul a great flexibility of movement. The relationship which must have quickly developed between Publius and his prisoner/guest would have encouraged this factor considerably. We are told that 'honors' were liberally given. This leads us to think that rather than spend his time in a Rabat cave, Paul was feted more and more until the time came for the final lavish farewell gifts from grateful people. Given the freedom visualised however, and Rabat being the greatest concentration of population and knowing his evangelical appetite, we can be fairly confident that Paul spent much time there to justify the later pilgrimages in the early Christian centuries. That a shrine of St. Paul existed at San Pawl Milqi before 381AD we know, for it was taken over by the Church of Malta following the decrees of Theodocius I. If the shrine did not belong to the Church before this date then presumably it was maintained by the descendants of the Publius family. It is these intervening centuries whose silence is so intriguing. The lack of early church buildings or conspicuous hierarchy obscures the fact of a quietly growing Christian Church.

The weather in the winter months would have provided few problems for a man who had suffered so many extremes. Even on the coldest days in Malta's mild climate it is unlikely that he would have been missing the cloak he had left at Troas. Later, when he was in Rome, he was to ask Timothy in a letter to bring it to him for the winter in that colder latitude.[12] One can imagine that a grateful Publius would have seen that he was provided for. Gazing at the rocky landscape, Paul would marvel at the industry of the people who could snatch so many crops from so little soil in such a dry land.

After years of constant journeyings and harassment, he could enjoy the peace of dwelling among a hospitable people and spend his time caring for them and pronouncing the faith which was the inspiration of his life.

Paul's convincing style had sincerity as its base. He spoke of a religious experience which had utterly transformed his life. Theological argument seldom grips the listener but personal experience vividly described will always hold an audience. What Paul succeeded in doing was to relate his experience to spiritual depths within the listener. When he told of the words of Jesus which had challenged and won his allegiance they knew that it had really happened. This man had found life of a quality that seemed to turn his manacles into medals of honour that he seemed proud to wear because they enabled him the better to serve the Christ who had commissioned him. In an insecure world haunted by superstitious dread here was a man who pronounced a living faith, who offered a place in the present and the future. The Divine Jesus who had transformed him would one day come to them also if they made themselves ready. And those recognised as being ready were invited to the Table of the Lord, the Agape of Christ, there to partake of the bread and the wine and utter the Maranatha (O Lord Come).

The sort of worship Paul demonstrated would become the pattern of worship for the adherents of the new faith. The remembering of Christ in the breaking of bread that we come across in Paul's epistles would become the customary observance of the Maltese Christians. The occasions and places for this to take place would also develop in the course of time.

When the time drew near for Paul to depart to Rome on the 'Castor & Pollox' there would be the question in the mind of Publius as to how far he might be able to help Paul with his case before Caesar. Perhaps there were letters of recommendation by the hand of the centurion, possibly the offer to travel to Rome to speak on Paul's behalf.

It is the years that followed that must now invite our attention. People live and people die. A generation carries on a tradition of its fathers, experiments with new ideas and sometimes leaves behind tangible memorials of its achievements. Alas, in Malta there is not a lot to be seen above the ground of the industry of these early Christian centuries. The stones that Paul's generation raised up to build this and that were used by later generations to develop new schemes. Many of the treasures were pillaged by successive invaders and reached some distant shore, to be admired by idle gazers there who were never to know the heartbeat of the Maltese people. What they could not take away was the story which the Maltese have carved within the living rock itself. The history of the early Christian centuries is in its rock-cut tombs.

From the beginning we have taken special note of the people who hurried to the aid of the shipwrecked travellers and have made out a case for their having come from the settlement at Beniarrad. In a later section, for those interested in considering detail, we shall examine more closely the Salina Bay catacombs – the burial ground of the people of Beniarrad. We would like to think that some are tombs of people who met Paul. It is surely true that the burial ground contains tombs of people who in their successive generations saw the decline of Roman power and the replacement of Greek by Byzantine culture. These were centuries which saw the blossoming of Christianity from the furtive early days of persecution to the days when its adherents could freely express their faith until the Arab invasion changed the whole outlook of the island.

THE EARLIEST CHURCHES

We do not know how large the population of Melita was when Paul was there, nor do we know the administrative structure. The wide ditch around Rabat and later, the round towers indicate a garrison. Army personnel, though perhaps few in number, would be conspicuous and Julius the centurion would no doubt find his place in military circles during those winter months. Many tales would have been told of the campaigns which each had been engaged in and the countries they had visited.

In trying to visualise the life-style of the days of Paul we have to forget completely the routine of modern civilisation with its forty hour week and leisured weekends. In the days of Roman control there was nothing comparable with our regular Saturday sport and relaxed Sunday. As slaves, a high proportion could never be free to plan their own lives. As property of their Master they were limited by his requirements. The free citizen often found that the burden of taxation necessitated a curtailment of free time.

As Paul once wrote 'not many wise, not many mighty, not many noble are called'[13] from which we gather that the members of the first Christian Churches were mainly from the poorer, less educated sections of the community. Such people would be more difficult to organise into churches by reason of the restrictions on their availability. That is probably one of the reasons why they met at the beginning and end of the day for their worship. That was when they could be free from unavoidable duties. No 11am and 6.30pm services for them!

There is not the slightest doubt that there were considerable social and domestic problems arising from the desire of a convert to attend gatherings of Christians. The unconverted husband would be unlikely to permit his Christian wife to slip away to the 'agape' or 'love feast' that wicked tongues were soon to misinterpret. The slave concubine could not change her status just because she had become a Christian. Roman Law was quite clear on the obligations of slaves and Church Law had soon to make pronouncements on such issues.

Paul was well aware of these problems and would be concerned. He had to plan for the future instruction of his converts. The basic facts of the Christian faith must be implanted without delay. Some must be set aside for special instruction to enable them to deal with the inevitable theological questions which would follow both from converts sincerely seeking to learn more and from cynics concerned only to ridicule.

Here again Malta provided an unusual factor. Whereas in all his other missionary work he had a flexible time-scale, in Malta the period available was firmly set. He had only until the end of winter when the sailing season re-opened. He knew how much time was available almost to the day. A ship bound for Rome was already anchored for the winter. Centurion Julius had booked passages on it. When that ship sailed, Paul would have to leave Malta.

Whether confined at Rabat, or Wardija, or free to move about the island under guard, his sense of commission would impel him to do certain things. Here was an evangelist who had founded many churches over the years, who had encountered opposition of every kind and been subjected to much indignity and painful treatment. How was a prisoner, with only three months available, to establish a church in Malta? The answer seems to be that he had a team with him.

Apart from the preparation of people as individuals, there was also the necessity of arrangements for groups, and therefore meeting places. The basic fundamentals of what was meant by a Christian church would have to be made clear. Paul had experienced difficulty before when immature adherents or worse had upset the pattern of the church he had founded as evidenced by his heart-felt letters to Corinth and elsewhere. Let us look therefore at what can be discovered about the nature of the earliest Christian churches.

About the same time as Paul was in Rome, Pliny the Younger was born. At the end of the century he wrote reporting a legal investigation concerning the habits of Christians:

> "They declared that the sum of their guilt or error had amounted only to this, that on an appointed day they had been accustomed to meet before daybreak and to recite a hymn antiphonally to Christ, as to a god, and to bind themselves by an oath . . . after the conclusion of this ceremony it was their custom to depart and meet again to take food but it was ordinary and harmless food."

This is a very interesting journalistic comment for it provides certain basic facts unclouded by the religious bias of an adherent.

Throughout the years of his evangelical tours, Paul founded churches wherever he went. Copies of the letters he sent to some of them still survive. There must have been many other Pauline churches whose names are forgotten and which will never be known. We know the pattern which he followed when he worked in fresh territory. The units he established in Malta would be similar to those in Greece and Asia Minor. The type of worship to which Paul was accustomed would be the type of worship which the Maltese Christians would follow. As Paul had drawn crowds to the lecture hall at Ephesus, the agora at Corinth and the Theatre at Perga,[14] so, if permitted, he would use a public place in Rabat. That the people came to him is a stated fact in a historical document. That the people who came were influenced is clear from the fact that he was showered with gifts when he left.

The holding of public meetings however was one thing, but the training of converts and the nature of their devotional sessions is perhaps in a different category. The practice would surely be as at Antioch or Troas. He would gather them together in someone's house though it be but a cave dwelling.

A characteristic which the Acts of the Apostles reveals about Paul is his custom of going to the synagogue on arrival in new surroundings, if one existed. This, and his following Jewish requirements when visiting Jerusalem only two years earlier, clearly demonstrate that his worship retained much that was Jewish.

Canon Streeter in 'The Primitive Church' points out that for the first fifty years the conception of the church was as the 'remnant' of Israel and of the Prophets and that the place where Christians met for worship is actually called a synagogue in the Epistle of James. 11. v 2. and in Hermas. He also points out that the weekly worship found expression in the Eucharist. That Christianity was born out of Judaism is a fact of history and it is not surprising therefore that in the earliest days, Christians were able to enjoy the privileges granted to Jews. This in itself indicates that their worship must have had sufficient in common with Judaism for the authorities to see little distinction.

The synagogue service consisted of prayer, the reading of the Law and prophets usually followed by explanation of the meaning of the reading and the Blessing. A characteristic of the service was the way in which any member of the congregation might take part regardless of whether they belonged to the privileged class. The Christian Hippolytus, writing something over a century after Paul, looks back to the way in which things were done in his youth and refers to the 'Apostolic Tradition'. It would seem from this document that his initiation into the Christian faith was similar to the initiation of Jewish proselytes, as was the baptismal rites. The 'sealing' rite, which we would now call confirmation, was equivalent to circumcision for the Jew.

It has to be remembered that to the end Paul was a Jew. He never renounced his Judaism or the things he had been taught as a boy and later as an ardent Pharisee. In Jesus Christ he had found a new dimension to his Jewish faith. Christ embodied all that to which the Patriarchs and Prophets had been pointing. Jesus was the awaited Messiah. Paul had been converted by this realisation and as a result had found a new power that thereafter was his driving force.

The sort of worship Paul demonstrated would become the pattern of worship for the adherents to the new faith. The remembering of Christ in the breaking of bread that we come across in Paul's epistles would become the customary observance of the Maltese Christians. The occasions and places for this to take place would develop as circumstances allowed. From the foregoing we may gather that the earliest churches were of a synagogue type. There is no reason for believing that Maltese churches would have been different with Paul as their founder.

As it was far too early for the erection of special buildings to be considered, unless cut into the rock, we have to consider where, in fact, the converts were to meet. Although Jewish tombs have been found no signs of early synagogues have been discovered. The custom of meeting 'from house to house' referred to in the New Testament would probably have limited application in the largely rural conditions of Malta and the problem of status cannot be overlooked entirely. The slave could not be host. The cave-dwelling peasant could not offer accommodation of a type to which they would feel they could invite the aristocracy to share in the Lord's Supper. The aristocracy, for their part, whose premises were eminently suitable, might not consider it proper to invite the slaves and freemen associated with someone else of standing in the community. In early days separate churches might develop in the same community for such domestic reasons. Paul addressed his letters usually to churches in specified towns but he also wrote 'to the church in thy house' when he wrote to Philemon.

But where in Malta are the Christian meeting places of early Christian centuries? The only evidence of Christianity that we can find from the Roman period is in the tombs. This point will be pursued later in the section on the Agape.

As far as the continuance of the Christian Church in later centuries is concerned there is very limited evidence remaining from the first Christian centuries. When we realise that the Byzantine influence became so strong in the island, the information that the Maltese church appeared to have continued under the jurisdiction of Rome up to the Arab invasion is interesting. The reason is perhaps not hard to find. Paul founded this church. Paul always kept in touch personally with his churches and would no doubt have corresponded from prison in Rome. The communication having been established it would be a natural outcome for his fellow evangelists to continue to nurse the young church after Paul's death.

THE TEAM

We have already touched upon Paul's concern that the new converts should be instructed and if necessary organised. To achieve this he needed competent assistants. Ideally, someone needed to remain on the island when he departed in order to nurse a newly created church. To consider who his companions were we must go back again to the events in Jerusalem.

Few people doubt that it was Luke who described the events in the Acts of the Apostles and because the shipwreck story is written from the viewpoint of an eyewitness this would make him one of the companions.

At the beginning of the voyage Luke makes special mention of Aristarchus.[15] We know that he was a Macedonian of Thessalonica. The first time we hear of him was at a time of trouble in Ephesus, when he is named as one of Paul's travelling companions. As a result of Paul's preaching, there had been such a turning to Christianity, that people making their living out of the souvenir trade associated with the temple of Diana, feared that they might be put out of business. Agitators, stirring a mob into hysteria, filled the great theatre with chanting people. They took Aristarchus and his friend prisoner, while other leading town figures were managing to get Paul away to safety. The matter was sorted out and subsequently Aristarchus was part of the team that went to Europe and later accompanied Paul to Jerusalem. In his letter to the church at Collossae Paul refers to him as 'my fellow-prisoner in Jesus Christ' but this might be his expression for a 'committed Christian'. Whether or not he was also a prisoner the fact that interests us is that we know he was with Paul when the ship left Caesarea.

One fact of Roman law that we know about is that a prisoner was permitted to take two servants on a voyage of this kind. So long as they paid their fare and the captain agreed, there is no reason why others should not make the trip as passengers. It would be a matter of negotiation. Tertius,[16] for instance, who was Paul's secretary when he wrote to Romans three years earlier, may well have travelled with him thereafter.

An interesting point is that Luke does not say that only Aristarchus was with them. The New English Bible and other translations imply that he was one of the party. This allows us to contemplate a group of two or more in addition to Paul and the writer. Some commentators have suggested Titus.[17] Although he was not among the delegates to Jerusalem he could have joined Paul later at Caesarea.

There was one other who ought to have been with Paul and for a very important reason. Paul was arrested in Jerusalem because of the accusation that he had broken Jewish Law by taking a Gentile into the forbidden part of the Temple. The Gentile with him at the time of the arrest was Trophimus, a native of Ephesus where Paul had experienced trouble. If witnesses of any kind were to carry any weight at the trial in Rome the most important of all would be Trophimus, the man he was accused of having taken into the forbidden part of the Temple. This was the man above all others that he needed to have with him in Rome and therefore an obvious choice for a travelling companion.

One of the great problems for Biblical scholars is what happened to Paul after he had been in Rome for two years. It had been Paul's ambition to go on to Spain, but the fact that references in some of his later letters mention places that do not fit into earlier known journeys raises lots of questions.

Most scholars are agreed that the letters to Timothy as they stand could not have been written by Paul because they contain material which could only refer to the nature of the Christian church in a later century. This does not however exclude the possibility that fragment of Paul's original letters have been used to introduce later teaching and that the fragments most likely to have been Pauline are those which refer to his known companions.

Knowing that it had been his intention to go to Spain after his Jerusalem visit it is likely that the team to accompany him was already planned. Those involved would know about it because each would have to make the necessary arrangements to be free to travel. Timothy was not included. It had been made clear to him that his job was to remain at Ephesus. The final explanation of the plans would have been provided by Paul at Miletus when he sent for Timothy and the leaders of the Ephesian church to join in final discussions of what was to be done in Asia Minor while he was away in Rome and Spain. (Today a mosque stands on the site of the original Christian church of Miletus). It was there that Paul said his farewells to his Asian Christian friends.

That was the plan, but it did not work out. Paul's arrest and long imprisonment in Caesarea upset everything. The team was ultimately dispersed to undertake fresh responsibilities. In time messages would reach Timothy explaining what had happened.

It was much later that Paul wrote to him from Rome. In his letter he is updating him. In writing he refers to people Timothy might have expected to be still with him. Those not mentioned were presumably known by Timothy to be elsewhere. For the same reason when Luke writes to Theophilus[18] onlv Aristarchus is mentioned in Acts. because. written at a much later date he was the only companion to be accounted for as far as he was concerned. Theophilus would know about the rest. We notice, in fact, that Luke several times names the companions of Paul from the time of the trouble in Ephesus to the trouble in Jerusalem. To have named individuals and where they came from seemed to have importance.

What did the prison weary Paul write to Timothy? He explained that Demas had gone to Thessalonica and was lost. Crescens was in Galatia and Titus in Dalmatia and Erastus in Corinth. Only Luke is with him so he wants Timothy to bring Mark and on the way to bring the cloak he had left with Carpus at Troas. He explains that Tychicus is on the way to take over at Ephesus.[19]

Now comes a very interesting point – at the very end of the list explaining what had happened to the team Paul writes, "Trophimus I have left at Miletus, sick". Yet Miletus is so close to Ephesus where Timothy was in charge that it was not necessary for anyone to write all the way from Rome to tell him what was regional if not local news! This makes us look for an error somewhere.

We note that the emperor Claudius in AD49 had difficulty with 'Christos' and 'Chrestos' because of similarity of pronunciation of the Greek vowels. Is there anyone who has not had difficulty in reading someone else's writing and having to guess at the meaning and not learning what was originally intended? Is it not true that even the most modern presses sometimes produce a misprint or get letters in the wrong order? An expert once drew attention to Acts Ch 27 verses 7, 8 and 16 where the Greek 'molis' is confused with 'polis'. In a recent work by a well known author and a famous publishing house (and mentioned in my Bibliography) I had occasion to search the index for the reference 'Melitus'. I was directed to page 211. I was unable to find it but instead found the word 'Miletus'!

In the letter to Timothy the same sort of thing could well have happened particularly if the shorthand MLT had been used and someone could have transcribed a placename familiar to them rather than that of a small island they had perhaps never heard of. Miletus was one of the great cities of the day and would readily come to mind when in reality the message probably was 'Trophimus I left in Melita, sick'.

If this in fact happened it goes a long way to clearing the chronological problem mentioned earlier and has a bearing on the sort of provision Paul made for the development of the young Maltese church. The sick Trophimus could have offered to stay on to help until the message came that the date had been fixed for the trial in Rome.[20]

So the happy and restful three months stay in Melita would come to an end as the Spring flowers began to open and the day of departure arrived. It was most certainly an emotional scene at the quayside with the host of tearful, waving people and among them the converted Publius. Paul had been permitted a last moment of glorious satisfaction before facing the grim prospect which awaited him in Italy. He had left these hospitable people in good hands. Trophimus would guide them aright. So Paul would watch the honey-coloured rocks of Melita disappear into the distance and only the sea stretched before and behind him. A warrior was drawing near to the end of his journey. Around him on the deck the gifts a grateful people had showered upon him. It was worth the perils of a shipwreck to have met them and served them. He did not just leave a memory. He left a church.

In the courtyard alongside the ancient church of S. Paolo fuori le Mura in Rome, where Paul is said to have been buried after his martyrdom, amongst the Christian graffiti and other relics of Roman days, is a broken stone tablet, probably a burial inscription. It bears one word 'Trophimus'.

Salina catacombs: above, entrance B.

Catacomb B. Plan.

Denis de Luca

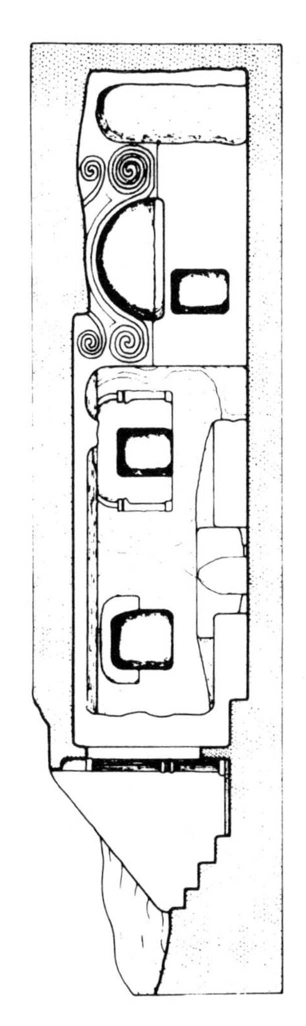

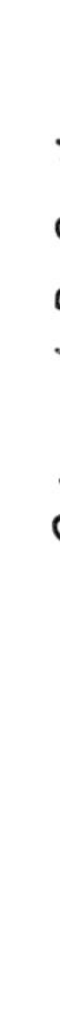

Catacomb B. Section *Denis de Luca*

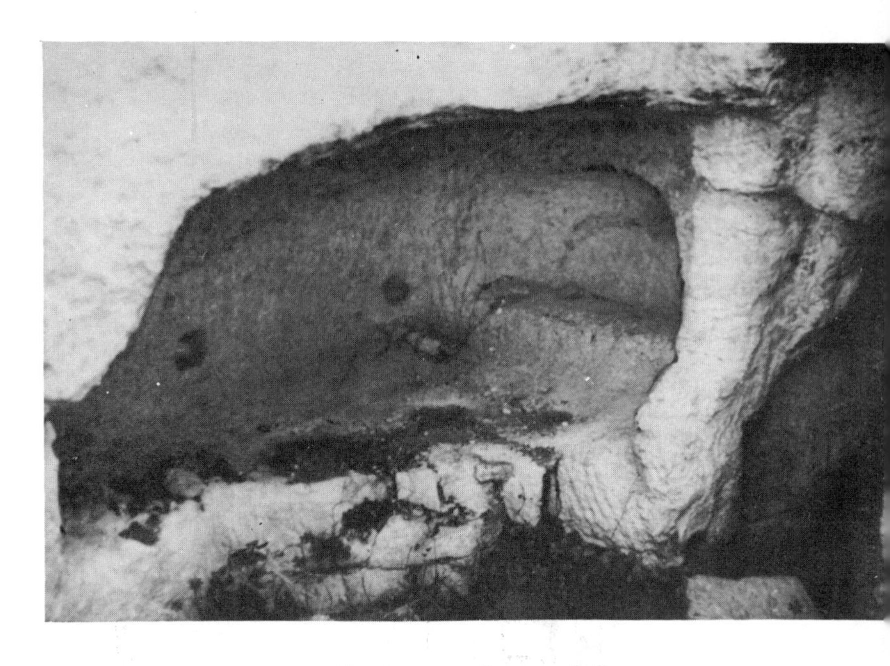

Tombs near salt pans. Salina

Floor graves

Salina catacombs: entrances E & F above: *A. Bon*

entrances D & E. (below.)

Salina catacombs: entrance C

below: showing child's loculus tomb

A. Bonano

inside unexcavated catacomb complex 0.

above: Christian graffiti. tomb under field:

A. Bonanc

Catacomb F. Agape table with tombs beyond.

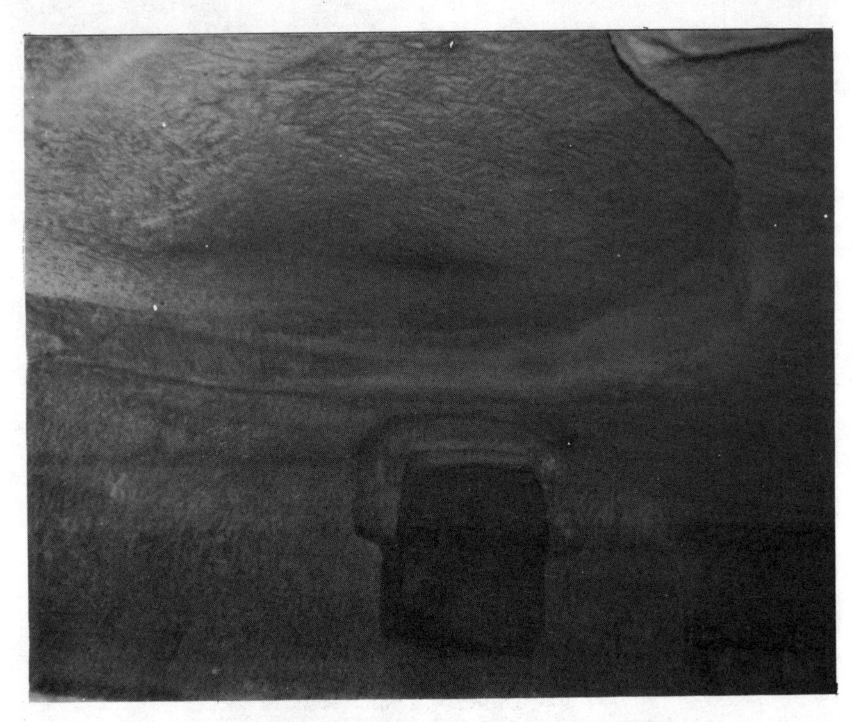

above: ceiling above Agape. catacomb B

below: catacomb D showing child's loculus tomb and bore hole.

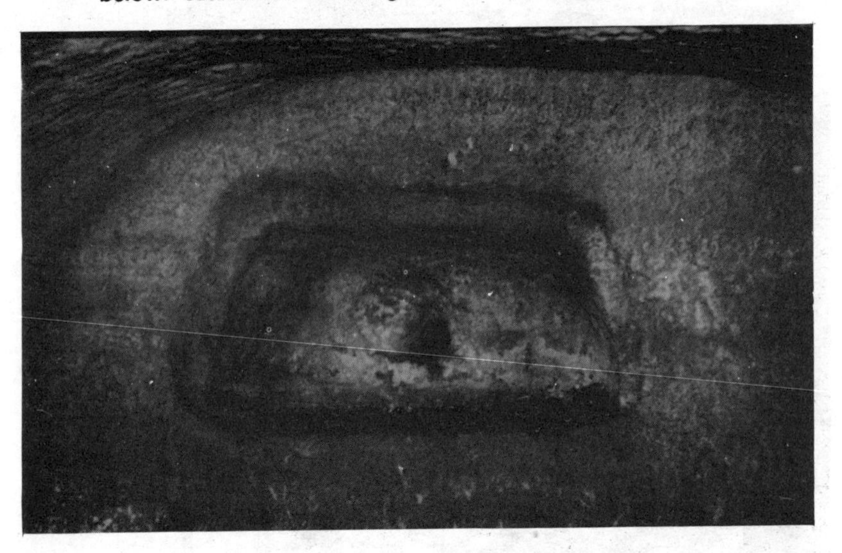

Christian symbols. catacomb B

below:

layout of Salina catacombs from scale model

right: tomb entrance near saltpans.

below. entrances N & M unexcavated.

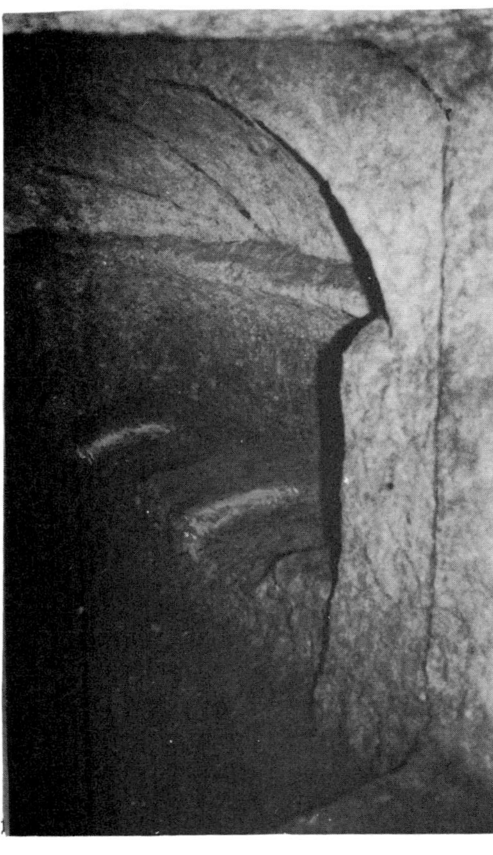

decorations inside tomb and headrests.

A. Bonano

Decorated tomb. catacomb B. note remains of column over Agape table

above: tomb decoration, catacomb B. below: agape, catacomb B

Wall carving. catacomb B

N
C
D
E
F
A approx 40 metres
B approx 20 metres
O approx 50 metres
X
N M L
K J I H G
0 50 100 200 300 400 500 CMS

SALINA CATACOMBS

Earlier, we paused to look at the cart-ruts by the Annunciata Chapel. Now let us look more closely at the tombs which were the last resting place of the generations who lived in that settlement in the early Christian centuries.

Walk up the lane beside the Chapel and in a matter of a few yards you reach the gate of the farmhouse. You may perhaps meet the farmer's wife who will gladly show you over the site.[21] She will tell you how her father-in-law Andrew Sammut in 1937, realising that the catacombs were worthy of examination, personally cleaned the mud from them and was able to supply tangible evidence to the Museum at Valletta. Now, his sons Vincent and Joseph farm the land and kindly permit visitors to wander over their fields to admire the memorials from the past – a gesture which tourists and visitors alike should appreciate.

Two separate tombs which were in the farm yard are now cemented over, but their position is important in enabling us to appreciate how widespread this burial ground was. The road itself almost certainly covers other tombs. We have already drawn attention to tombs above the cart-ruts. These are not now so easily identified because over a long period children have had great fun moving quantities of rocks to build fortresses around the entrances and some have been covered altogether. Building development in the area has destroyed or hidden others. Two house tombs are still to be seen and a group of three almost filled with earth.

In a quarried area lower down the hill and not far from the lay-by near the salt-pans there is a group consisting of one double and three single tombs from an early period, but these have been much refashioned for later use as a shelter. Closer to the bay along the same terracing another entrance has been blocked with stones. Scattered over this part of the hill at irregular intervals and with no obvious planning pattern are ten shallow floor graves. This would appear to have been an area where the residents of the settlement were buried before communal planning came into effect in the area adjacent to the Annuciata Chapel. The timing of the change to the planned burial areas may have coincided with the beginnings of the Christian faith in the island.

A gap in the wall opposite the farmhouse entrance permits access to the first narrow field above the chapel. Under the soil are floor graves. Under the trees to the left and beyond are a variety of shallow graves some of them believed to be punic from early in the days of Roman occupation. Punic refers to the period of Carthaginian control of the island before the Roman conquest but the punic influence lasted for a long time and burial styles would not quickly change.

The first thing to be realised is that this ancient burial ground is a hillside which has been carefully quarried to create terraces which at a later date, possibly at the time of the Knights, became fields. The narrow fields above the chapel are in the region of one hundred yards in length (and longer before modern houses were erected at the southern end). The line of the quarried terracing is parallel to the creek. The perpendicular walls resulting from the quarrying became the faces into which the tomb entrances were cut.

Our route so far has taken us across the soil of the narrow strip which is the first field. It is bordered by a wall of rocks along the line of the quarried face which is still to be seen here and there above the soil. As we walk from the road across the field we find a hole in the rock immediately in front of us. It has a drop of several feet onto the debris below and leads to an underground passage blocked at the far end. Only the fit and agile should explore this as it is difficult to climb back again. Any who venture should look closely at a tomb on the left hand side. Adjoining the spiral pillaster on the left hand side of the tomb clearly carved into the wall is an example of early Christian graffiti. It consists of a lamb, above which is a monogram of Christ and two Greek letters, which were symbols used by early Christians. The significance of these is that for the first centuries of the Christian era Greek was still the language commonly used. Alpha and omega represent the beginning and the end for these are the first and last letters of the Greek alphabet. In the book of the Revelation 1. v 8. the expression 'I am the Alpha and the Omega' means 'I am the first and the last'. Chi-Rho were an abbreviation of the first letters of the name of Christ. 'Ch' was written 'X' in Greek and 'R' as 'P' (Rho). The emperor Constantine before going into battle had a vision of the cross and got his soldiers to carry the Chi-Rho symbol into battle. Thereafter it came into common use by Christians.

Your attention is drawn to the plan on p 89 as an aid to a study of this fascinating site. The passage containing this Christian symbol either has an entrance mid-field or was entered at point NM on the plan.

The second field, which is about one hundred yards by about fourteen yards, seems quite a normal field until one examines the long quarried edge on the further side. Then, almost hidden by the level of the soil can be discovered the entrances to the tombs indicated on the plan. The only one which is easy of access is that marked G. It is entered by means of steps leading down and these give us some idea of the probable depth of the rock floor beneath the field. These steps were not put there, they were carved out of the living rock. All the tombs about to be described have been cut inch by inch from solid rock, and with very simple tools. One realises what a lot of hard patient work must have been involved for the inhabitants of Beniarrad. The tombs inside G are of a simple table type which were originally covered with a stone slab. This was probably a family vault. A sherd (a fragment of pottery) found there has been considered to be as early as the third century AD.

Tombs I and L are of a different type known as loculus tombs. These are virtually shelves which were sealed up by vertical stone slabs set into the rock face. The more adventurous, who do not mind squeezing through narrow apertures on their stomach, might be interested to crawl full-length on the soil to examine tomb J. Once inside one finds a passage with a single tomb immediately on the left. Some six feet further on a double tomb has been cut on the other side of the passage. Along the passage wall leading to it is a tapered groove which opens out into a domed hole about six inches high leading into the tomb chamber. Presumably this was a shelf for resting oil lamps to allow light to shine both in the passage and in the tomb chamber itself.

K is very intriguing because it is a passage leading into the hill, but there is a sturdy vine growing across the entrance which prevents investigation.

Perhaps the most interesting part of this level is at the far corner of the field where a carob tree hides the fact that a whole group of tombs are hidden by the soil which reaches to within a few inches of the top of the entrances. One unusual feature which excavation will reveal is the existence of a porch with a single pillar supporting the arches of two different entrances. See illustration. Under this second field are more floor graves.

Before we proceed to the main part of this ancient burial ground it should be pointed out that the word catacomb is an adaption of the Greek 'kata kymben' meaning 'near the dell'. The dell in question was an area near the ancient church of San Sebastian on the Appian Way, outside the walls of ancient Rome, and not places where Christians took refuge from persecution as many have been led to believe. The name, having been given to this particular burial ground came to be applied to similar underground groups of tombs. Those of Rome are thought to have been from the second to the fourth century AD. In Malta the cutting of rock tombs began much earlier.

Paul, in the course of his travels, would have seen tombs of many kinds in Asia and Greece, but the rock-cut tomb would not have been new to him. He would have seen them in Judea and Syria and Turkey. One of the last things he saw as the corn ship sailed away from Myra could have been the elaborately cut tombs in the cliff-face above the harbour, although some of these would be later. In Malta he would come across the punic tombs of earlier centuries. The Romans were in power but the punic style would remain. During his three months stay funeral ceremonies are bound to have taken place with traditional local rites. People would have been buried with domestic utensils, which is why pottery is found in ancient tombs. There is no reason to believe that Christian burial differed much in those early days. Customs do not quickly change. A converted Christian of that generation is still likely to have been buried according to the traditions of his family. The belief in the resurrection which Christianity brought would emphasise burial rather than the cremation practised by the Romans. There are no cremation urns in these catacombs, nor provision to house them.

We now proceed to the most conspicuous part of the burial ground which is on a higher terrace but is cut differently. Here a rectangle has been cut into the hill surrounded on all but the entrance side by tombs. Whether or not this rectangle was originally roofed over, it was cut before the tomb entrances which lead from it. To the right of this rectangle where the slope of the former hill remains, a number of shallow floor graves are to be seen cut into the hill slope. Apart from the entrances marked on plan 89 the remains of a number of individual floor and loculus tombs are to be seen, particularly high up on the right hand side where later quarrying has taken place.

At point C a carefully cut doorway leads down several steps to an 'L' shaped passage. On either side of the first section of the passage are canopied table graves arranged in series. They are called table graves because they are sealed by flat stones which give the appearance of a table top. In the branch passage there is an arcosolium. This type of tomb is cut into the wall and has an opening fashioned like a window. Behind the opening the tomb opens out with a flat floor of body length with a stone 'pillow' at one end into which have been cut two headrests. The ceiling above is domed. These headrests are typical of all except the loculus tombs in this burial ground. The nature of the cutting of this catacomb is somewhat crude and appears to be earlier than many described later. According to Harrison Lewis sherds dating from the second to fourth century AD have been found in this catacomb.[22]

Entrance D leads to a spacious chamber in the centre of which is a large canopied tomb. Although it is so irregularly cut its great size and considerable passageways all round marks it out as a tomb of some importance. The front wall has a window cut into it, but probably at a much later date. The other three walls each have large arcosolium tombs. An interesting feature of this catacomb is a stone seat near the entrance and at the back at shoulder height a projection near the left hand corner with a niche above it may have served as a pedestal.

Catacomb E is an exception to all the other entrances in that it is at a much higher level, is rounded above, and one has to stoop to enter. Inside, however, steps lead down to a floor level comparable with the others. The tombs here are similar to those in C but there are more of them and there is sufficient open space for a small company of people to gather. Remembering the slow process of tomb cutting, the loculus tombs here and in the open at intervals around the rectangle, may have been more quickly prepared for people who had died unexpectedly. Judging by the size some of them must have been children or the comparatively young for whom a planned resting-place was not available. Walking straight forward from the inner steps one finds on the left hand side at the rear a double tomb and linked to it a narrow trough-like child's tomb. An unusual feature is found in the wall at the back where a loculus tomb for a small child is obviously related to the parent tomb. The significance of the hole in the centre of it is discussed below. Another unusual feature of this catacomb is the fact that single tombs out-number the double by three to one. A predominant feature of the grouped or family tomb complexes at Salina is that they are nearly all double burials. On the wall outside entrance E is a deeply cut cross, though it is questionable whether this was there at the time these tombs were prepared.

Remembering that all the tombs were cut from the solid rock inch by inch, it is clear that they were developed over a considerable period. Assuming each catacomb to be either a family or cult burial ground it is interesting to note the care taken by D and E not to infringe each other's territorial rights. That E was begun earlier seems to be demonstrated by the fact that the passage of D bears away to the left before opening out into the main chamber. At a later date when the child's tomb was cut at the rear of the double tomb in E mentioned above, a test bore was made to ensure that there was no question of breaking into the adjoining catacomb D.

The largest catacomb of all, F on the plan, is distinguished by the agape table just inside the entrance. This feature will be discussed later. The central tomb at the far end facing the entrance has two crosses close together on the front face. This catacomb has a central space large enough for a gathering of upwards of fifty people in conjunction with the agape table.

The other catacombs on this section of the hill are distinguished by isolation. There are two, namely A and B, and they are several yards to the north. In the case of each it is necessary to go down several steps before reaching their respective entrances. Nevertheless the ceiling height and floor levels are similar to the catacombs around the rectangle.

Some deep 'cart-ruts' between these entrances prove the slope of this part of the hill before the tombs were cut. There are no signs of quarrying here and insufficient soil to call it a field, yet a heap of soil and debris once covered entrance B implying that there was a reason for covering the tomb entrance at some time. A, which has a short central passage which is rather narrow and has two tombs on either side, points east. That an underground passage of some kind exists in front of and below the entrance to tomb B is provable and probably has an entrance behind a pile of rocks in the field below.

It is catacomb B itself which outshines in interest everything else to be found in the Saline catacombs.

We get the impression that we are about to see something special as soon as we see the carved pillars, on each side of the doorway. Though crudely cut they are reminiscent of Roman architecture. If this door is locked the key is obtainable from the farmhouse. Inside we find beautiful examples of canopied saddleback tombs, a single grave and two arcosolii set in the wall behind another agape table. The wealth of decoration is in such a marked contrast to all the other tombs that its isolation from the rest seems to give it special significance. At least it would appear to be the property of a wealthy family for carved decoration is to be seen everywhere.

The study of Christian art begins with Christian tombs. Simple carvings were an attempt to convey a belief. As whole families became Christian it might have seemed appropriate to decorate their tombs with distinguishing marks which had come to be associated with the beliefs of the early church. Experts generally assert that Christian symbolism did not begin until persecution had come to an end with the emperor

Constantine in the early third century AD. Against this, of course, are isolated examples such as those found at Herculaneum, Dura-Europa etc. What found public expression after Constantine was probably concealed practice earlier by committed Christians. It does not seem strange for a Christian adherent to write or carve the symbol of a cross when Paul had written so passionately about it as early as 55AD and scribes had been busily copying such documents and handing them on from church to church.

Greek was the comon language of the Roman empire in Paul's day. The Greek word for fish was 'ixthus'. The letters of this Greek word are the first letters of Jesus Christ Son of God, Saviour, therefore a picture of a fish became a code for Christ. There would seem to be greater scope for a code sign during a time of persecution than after persecution had come to an end!

Let us now examine catacomb B carefully. The agape table is on the left hand side on entry. Above it, at eye-level, just inside the door is an upright cross. Look immediately to the right and on the passage wall behind the wooden door you will see a crude carving of a stag, a symbol of Divine Grace. This is at the head end of a single tomb which is at right angles to all the others. Move a few paces along the passage and facing the agape table is a saddle-backed canopied tomb with considerable decoration both inside and out. A predominant feature is a herringbone pattern and on the right hand side what appears to be an attempt to portray the top of a corinthian column.

The remaining tomb on the right hand side of the passage is conspicuous for its deeply cut crosses. On the left is a panel at the bottom of an arch which has a cross like an X. On the right, at the other end of the arch is a wheel cross. A few inches from this and facing the doorway is another slightly smaller.

Facing this tomb on the other side of the main passage is the most highly decorated tomb of all with elaborate scroll work along its entire length. At the end nearest the agape table there is an arched niche with spiral colonettes within which is what appears to have been a dolphin with a basket of loaves above it. This niche has the appearance of a shrine. On the lower face is some evidence of carved lettering.

Several tombs in the Salina catacombs have these spiral colonettes as part of their decoration either supporting canopy arches or inside the tomb itself. Although more crudely carved they are reminiscent of third century sarcophagi in the Antalya Museum, Turkey and in St. Peter's Necropolis, Rome.

Perhaps the most remarkable feature of catacomb B however, is the carving at the far end of the passage. I drew attention to it in 1975 and now that the mud has been removed from the deepest crevices it appears to be a group with a central figure. It is a remarkable conception by the artist for it must have been quite striking in its original form when the afternoon sun struck it as the door was opened. I imagine it to be associated with St. Paul. The torso of a man is clearly to be identified as well as folds of drapery.[23]

What is the earliest date we can give to the graffiti, decorations and carvings in the Salina tombs? Most experts tell us that they cannot be earlier than the third century which leads us to ask what are the earliest to have been found anywhere?

We have already referred to the fourth century ivory diptych and we know that in the same century there was a great deal of painting of the portraits of saints. St. Augustine affirmed that many persons reverenced sepulchres and paintings. We know Christian art existed in the reign of Constantine and the discovery of the house church at Dura-Europa reveals the existence of Christian art a century earlier. Andre Graber in his 'Christian Iconography' (Princetown University Press), adjudges the funerary cycles and the paintings at Dura as the very first Christian iconography. In his book he shows extensively that Christian art followed the pattern and characteristics of the art current in that day. A visitor to the second century catacombs around Rome will see depicted by artists people of that era reclining at tables provided with bread, wine and fish.

As far as Christian symbols and graffiti are concerned there are some writers who offer evidence of an early date. Jack Finegan in his 'Light from the Ancient Past' tells of the chamber tomb discovered and excavated in 1945 beside the road to Bethlehem near the Talpioth suburb of Jerusalem. In the tomb were four rectangular stone burial chests which have been dated earlier than 70AD because of a coin of

Agrippa I and pottery of late Hellenistic and early Roman style. Two of the chests have Greek inscriptions which could be classified as Christian. The fourth chest has on each of its four sides a rough cross, like a plus sign. In the pottery section at the Cathedral Museum, Mdina can be seen a terra-cotta oil lamp which is claimed to be from the first century AD which bears on its upper surface a very clearly moulded Cross. Most experts are sceptical of this early date claim.

He also tells us of a first century burial place on the Mount of Olives, in the vicinity of the Franciscan chapel, where on the ossuary bearing the name 'Judah the proselyte of Tyre' there is a monogram Chi Rho, another Iota, Chi, Beta and finally a carefully drawn cross. Possible evidence is also supplied in the upper room of the so-called 'bicentenery house' in Herculaneum, where is to be seen a somewhat irregular depression roughly in the form of a Latin cross. J. G. Davies in his 'Evangelism in the Early Church' suggests that the position of the nailmarks may indicate that the Christian occupant had snatched the cross from the wall before the rising mud and lava engulfed the town in August AD79.

How far we can use these examples to suggest that the use of Christian symbols was more widespread than we have been led to believe is debatable but one thing is clear. If the cross and Christian symbols were not used where they could be publicly seen in the first century, Paul and other evangelists clearly brought the cross to the attention of their listeners. Reference to it in his letters were copied and sent from church to church from the earliest times in the Churches' history. We cannot imagine Paul, now near the end of his ministry, not preaching to the Maltese about the cross. That persecution of Christians was to begin in Rome within a few years is indisputable and that it spread to big cities around the Mediterranean is also a known fact, but evidence of it in Malta is not obvious. In the years immediately after Paul's death who was to instigate the persecution if Publius was still Chief Man? He had himself, we are told, become a Christian. As for the people themselves they were so grateful for what Paul had done that they would not easily be encouraged to persecute the friends of this man. Some considerable time would have to elapse and some strong cultural force would be necessary, after the demise or removal of Publius, before another generation would be ready to denounce its own kin among the hospitable Maltese. We have already suggested that the change may have taken place at the time of the imposition of the Municipium.

The Christian symbolism of the Salina catacombs, and particularly in tomb B may have to be associated with later centuries. The creation of the Maltese See in 533AD may have triggered off the growth of Christian art in the island. Nevertheless we must not rule out the fact that from a time as early as Talpioth and Dura-Europa and Herculaneum there may have been devoted Christians who wished to express their faith with a graving tool on stone, even in Malta.

In Malta's hot climate burials could not be long delayed. As the cutting of the tomb chambers involved a slow and laborious job with somewhat primitive tools, there was no possibility of completing the work in a day or two unless a shallow surface grave was cut in the open (floor graves) or loculus (in walls). As far as catacombs with passages were concerned advanced preparation would be necessary. For this reason among others people would prepare their own tombs or have them prepared during their life time. This would account for the fact that not all tombs at Salina are completed. In B are two unfinished tombs which adds weight to the belief that the decoration on them was not added at a later date. The only main tomb in this catacomb which is finished has a deep groove above the line of the sealing stone. This was either a libation channel or was chipped out by vandals in forcing the stone to search for possible treasure within.

Just outside the entrance to catacomb D a group of seventy nine sherds were found. They varied very greatly in type but were adjudged to be chiefly fifth century AD with Byzantine characteristics. Some however, were thought could be as early as third century AD. Pieces of an oil lamp were of an African pattern, one fragment clearly shows part of a design. Such a variety being jumbled together in one place indicates a tomb clearance at some time, possibly dropped by grave robbers. These sherds bear out the view that these tombs are from the early Christian centuries. Harrison Lewis in his book 'Ancient Malta' goes further and claims that sherds have been found nearby in the rectangle which could have been as early as the first and second centuries AD.

We can conjecture therefore, that we are dealing in one site, with the generations which saw the flourishing of Roman rule, the split of the empire and the emergence of 'open' Christianity after years of 'furtive' adherence to their faith. Beniarrad seems to have sufficient tombs spread over the hill to account for a settlement of some ten families for a period of approximately five Christian centuries. When we were discussing the possible age of the tombs Mr. F. S. Mallia, Director of the Museum Department, Valletta, suggested that some may have been reused as is known to have happened elsewhere. In this case the community would have been larger.

THE RECTANGLE

Reference has been made earlier to the portion of the burial ground significantly cut differently from the rest, namely the rectangle from which catacombs C, D, E and F lead. This rectangle poses some interesting problems. First of all, why was it cut differently, as a rectangle, and not continued along the hill as a terrace as was the case in the fields below?

D. H. Trump in his 'Archeological Guide to Malta' has suggested that the stone was quarried from this site to build the Annunciata chapel. Local experts have disagreed on the grounds that a different type of stone was used for the chapel, viz, from the Madleina area. The fact that the chapel was not built until the seventeenth century and sherds more than a thousand years older have been found on the site, seems to bear out their objections. The quarry marks noticed by Trump are unmistakeably there and can be seen as deep cuts and shallow grooves.

The question of the reason for the rectangle leads to the problem of how access was originally gained to it. Reference to the site plan and photograph on page 83 will be an asset.

The rocks and debris inside the rectangle and the soil in the field below which hides the wall face of the terrace make it difficult to reach firm decisions regarding the nature of the floor levels. Today a passage cut in the rock at point X leads on to the soil of the field. But this would have had little purpose before the soil was put there as there would have been a drop of from six to eight feet. A deeper section in the central foreground could indicate an internal entrance from the lower level.

The scale model illustrated on p 83 is an attempt at rediscovering the former geography of this rectangle. The most obvious conclusion to justify X as the original entrance is that it was in use at a time when the hillslope continued uninterrupted to give easier access to users at this point. This would mean that the rectangle was in existence before this terrace was quarried.

That we are looking at its original floor shape is clear from a number of clues. On the left hand side of entrance C is a small child's loculus tomb and the marks where the sealing slab originally enclosed it. This is set in the wall above a block of stone which has the appearance of a seat. This must have been there before the tomb was cut. Judging by the stone removed from the roof of the catacomb behind it this wall must have been about two feet higher at this point. The corner to the right of entrance C higher up also once had a child's loculus tomb, but now all that remains is the bottom sill which housed the sealing stone (in which a tethering hole has been later cut). This helps us to establish the original height, for it brings it into line with the loculus tombs high up on the other side of the rectangle near entrance E, some of which have been quarried at a later date.

That the rectangle walls were not cut after the entrances to the catacombs, is clear from the fact that each has a sill which has to be surmounted before stepping down to the common floor level. In most cases, also, there is evidence that at some stage, doors blocked the entrances, indicating private ownership and emphasising that these were either family tombs or tombs of funeral clubs. Some of the doorways show evidence of where its door hung and how it was secured. The purpose of the steps down into the catacombs was presumably to establish sufficient height from floor to ceiling, ensuring a safe thickness in the roof formed by the hillside rock itself.

It would seem either that a quarry was taken over for the purpose of burials, or that this section of the hill was quarried to a plan which had burials in minds, or that it was cut for some communal purpose and tombs later cut round the perimeter. Supporting the planned theory is the fact that the line of the field terracing has, at a number of points, angled deviations carefully cut which break the straightness of the general line. The angles are clear and distinct and at each of these angles are passages or tomb entrances. This feature happens too often to be accidental. With method in the field boundaries we would expect method in the arrangement of the area surrounded by catacombs C to F.

We note that the wall face containing entrance C does not continue in an unbroken line towards the field but that the seat-like stone already mentioned is extended forward and points towards entrance F on the far side. We note also that entrance E is at a much higher level. This would seem to indicate some special feature under the debris piled immediately beneath it, e.g another tomb, platform or ceremonial object.

The corner adjoining entrance E has a projecting rounded shape and two parallel markings above the floor grave on its right. On the outside wall of catacomb D is a niche reminiscent of those in the first century remains beneath the church of San Clemente in Rome. Whether there is significance in all these things to indicate that the rectangle was used for ceremonial purposes can only be judged when there has been an adequate excavation of the site.

The fact that the emperor Septimus Severus in the last decade of the second century (180-200AD) permitted common cemeteries may help in our dating of the Salina tombs. The transition seen at Salina, from haphazard surface burials to planned areas, may have been around and after this date and bears some comparison with the sherds examined. That some cemeteries did exist at an earlier date is known. Another fact is that by 200AD Christian burial requirements had reached a stage where it was expected that the burial of the faithful should not be contaminated by pagan neighbours, which might give an added explanation for the isolation of the rectangle from the rest of the burial ground. That the tombs should be arranged around this rectangle implies special significance for the shape and gives us the impression of a meeting place. The position of this quarried area makes it inconspicuous from the bay or creek.

It is perhaps significant that the intensification of the persecution of Christians coincided with an era when the behaviour of Christians was of a nature which was tending to isolate them from the rest of the community.

THE AGAPE

We have left till last the study of the agape tables and their function, because it is a subject about which there is a great deal of conjecture.

To start with, it is best to describe what they look like. The first thing is that they are only found in catacombs and are cut from the living rock. Their size, wherever they are found in Malta, is fairly constant. In the case of those in Rabat, the surrounding rock has been cut away, possibly so that a greater number of people could be accommodated, but at Salina the tables at B and F respectively are both on the left hand side close to the entrance and cover a circular area some twelve feet in diameter and spaciously domed above and around. Each has a straight front edge formed by the passage itself. At Rabat, although the surroundings have been cut away, the straight front is also there, from which we may assume the shape was planned.

The tables themselves are about two feet high and marked from the surrounding rock by a raised stone circle some three feet in diameter. From this circle the rock slopes away to the wall allowing for a seating or reclining area. Within the circle the rock is flat, like a table. The circle is broken at one point where a niche in the straight front edge joins it. In the case of catacomb B there is a more elaborate variation inasmuch as beside the niche there are two low stone seats.

Because agape tables are to be found only in catacombs the assumption has been that they must be associated with burials and memorials to the dead. This is the view expressed by tourist guides and most textbooks on Malta. That they are not 'laying-out' tables is clear by the very shape of the surface with its raised circle and lack of easy access other than from the front.

There seems to be no dispute about the fact that the area within the circle constitutes the table, that the niche at the front housed a receptacle and that the break at the front of the circle above the niche was for clearing the remnants of the meal into the receptacle. It is the purpose of the meal and the nature of the ceremony where interpretations vary. There are no Maltese documents on the subject, so we have to search among writers elsewhere for information which may be of help.

Agape was Greek for love or affection. It was the custom in the early Christian Church for a comradely feast to be held which came to be called the agape or love feast. Archibald Robinson in 'The origin of Christianity' says that all the evidence points to its association with the Lord's Supper or Eucharist.

E. H. Broadbent in 'The Pilgrim Church' maintains that the origin for the regulation of the agape was Jewish, was derived from the period when most Christian leaders were Jewish by birth or upbringing or habit of mind, which in itself indicates a very early period in the history of the Church. That the Jews of the first century AD had charity feasts is a known fact of the Roman world. That Christians adopted the practice is easy to understand. That the Jewish and early Christian custom was not a meaningless banquetting club can be certain. No expert on early church history has yet been able to disentangle the evidence concerning the ritual of the commemorative supper of the Lord from the social gathering of the adherents until a later period. The reference in Acts 2. v 46 to the 'breaking of bread from house to house' probably included both in the Lord's Supper. In 1 Corinthians II v 20-34 Paul rebukes the members of the church at Corinth for unseemly behaviour at the meal and proceeds to refer to the last Supper of Jesus and the significance of the bread and the wine as a memorial. It would seem that the serious memorial meal was becoming too much of a social occasion.

The Epistle of Jude verses 12, and 2 Peter verse 13, also make reference to Love feasts. Ignatius of Antioch writing to the church at Smyrna about 112AD obviously included the Eucharist in the agape. Justin, writing about 150AD refers to the bread and wine and water and says 'This food is called with us the Eucharist' and after explaining the origin of the Last Supper of Jesus and the meaning of the symbolic remembrance, goes on to talk of fellowship and common sharing, Tertullian tells of:

> "The participants, before reclining tastes first of prayer to God. As much is eaten as satisfied the cravings of hunger: as much is drunk as befits the chaste . . . After manual ablutions and bringing in of lights, each is asked to stand forth and sing, as he can, a hymn to God, either from the Holy Scriptures or one of his own composing. This is a proof of the measure of our drinking. As the feast commenced with prayer, so it is closed with prayer".

In the catacombs of Rome, one of the scenes frequently depicted in early Christian art is the feast with reclining figures around a semi-circular table which has a raised edge, presumably cushions, and a straight front. On the half-circle table are loaves and fishes and sometimes wine. In the church of St. Domitilla beside the Appian Way, there is a marble table-top with a rim like a tray, almost identical in size with the centre circle cut into agape tables at Salina. When I enquired if this was an early agape table I was told that it was thought to be.

It would appear that special triclinia (three sided couches) were constructed around the agape tables for the participants with the President on the remaining side. The Salina agape tables seem to be following this pattern in stone. Because they are found in catacombs the idea of 'wakes' and anniversary feasts in memory of the dead has been the most readily accepted. This does not eliminate the possibility that it could have been used by small gatherings of Christians for observing the Eucharist or agape meal. That there is a similar pattern in all the agape tables of Malta is significant in itself.

A family 'wake' surely, would have provided scope for a variety of patterns according to family taste; The Maltese agape tables on the other hand have a remarkable similarity as if not only to fulfil a function, but also a ritual requirement. It is interesting that the size of the circle and its surround determined the number who can sit around it at one time, a 'synagogue' of twelve, perhaps?

Accepting the view that tombs were cut in advance of death whenever possible, the catacomb at B obviously had a plan of operation. Of necessity the cutting had to begin at the entrance with the main passage. It is therfore significant that the feature cut nearest to the entrance is not a tomb but the agape chamber. If this was not cut before any of the tombs we have to explain why so large an area of rock was left uncut remembering the laborious nature of the cutting process, in order to start cutting tombs at a greater distance from the entrance. With so much hard work involved and having already noticed that there was no time to complete all the tombs, the agape seems to assume an importance greater than the tombs. Why should so large a proportion of the total area be put aside for this chamber? Obviously it was intended for use. The circle in the centre of the rock table indicates that people sat around this circle. The straight front edge and niche draws attention to this point of the chamber, presumably because this is where the officiator stood.

When we look at the beginnings of Christianity in Jerusalem our starting point is an empty tomb and the proof of the success and vitality of the religion which evolved is adherents gathered around a communion table remembering the Christ who called them. The only evidence of early Christianity yet found in Malta is in the tombs and significantly it is there that we find the agape table, symbolic of communion.
Russell Meiggs in his 'Roman Ostia' expressed the opinion that for the first two and a half centuries Christians met and worshipped in cemeteries. We know that it was a characteristic of the age, with other religions as well as Christian, for memorial meals to be held at the graveside and had been since much earlier times.

Another factor which has to be borne in mind is the fact that before 200AD Christian buildings did not and could not exist. It was not permitted. Burial grounds gave scope for meeting which was otherwise limited to house gatherings. That the celebration of the agape led to abuses is known from the concern expressed by a number of church leaders at various times and it came to be discouraged. As this was at the end of the third century it would seem, contrary to expert opinion, that this was not when they were cut but when they ceased to be cut.

If the agape chambers are to be classified as rooms set aside for memorials to the Christian *dead*, where are the meeting places for the Christian *living* in that early period of the history of the church? That there must have been meeting places goes without saying and a growing church would need more accommodation as time went on. That the early church met 'from house to house' we know from the earliest Christian writings but in Malta apart from the aristocracy, the homes of the average Maltese would have hardly sufficed for the purpose of a Christian synagogue. Did they meet in caves to provide their table of the Lord and observe the communion meal? If they carved ritual tables for the dead, which are still to be seen, why do we not find similar ritual objects where living Christians celebrated their living faith? In those centuries, could it be that they served both purposes? To put it another way, did the Christian burial places develop around the spots associated with Christian ceremonial and teaching? In Rome and elsewhere we continually find that Churches have developed on the site of a burial ground of a highly esteemed Christian leader.

Is it not more in the spirit of the early Christians that because the Eucharist was central to their faith they wished, in death, to be close to the agape table which symbolised it? Is it not true that in cutting into the rock to create the catacombs, it is the Agape table which is close to the door and the tombs arranged around and beyond it?

An interesting point which could bear this out is apparent from the order of the cutting process in catacomb B. Originally the agape must have had its own chamber similar to that in F. On the left hand side of the chamber the wall adjoining the doorway has been shaped to represent a pillar or post to support the span above the front section of the agape. Examine the ceiling at the far end of the agape and we see the remnants of what must have been a corresponding feature at the other end of the span when the original wall on the right hand side was in existence. The wall has been removed but this fragment remains in the ceiling. We also notice that this fragment forms part of an arch further down the passage; this arch leads into a side passage cut later. When we study the ceiling of the agape itself we see a bold semi-circular rim corresponding with the agape floor shape. This ceiling rim joins up the two points mentioned, giving final proof of the shape of the original agape chamber. That this chamber was later enlarged is clear from a change in direction of the rear part of the wall which has been straightened. The right hand side of the agape chamber has been entirely removed either to establish a larger congregating area or to provide light for the magnificent saddleback tomb beyond the side passage which was cut later. That the cutting is later, is clear from the fact that the artist when completing his decoration of the side of this tomb, had to cramp part of his scroll pattern, because the arch which connects it to the agape chamber had already been cut and took up part of his design space. The point being made is that the agape seems to be older than the tombs associated with it. The only completed tombs are those near the door on the other side of the main passage.

A further point regarding the use of the Maltese agape tables is this. The era of persecution brought stricter application of the laws against meetings. Exemption was given to funeral clubs and memorial ceremonies in burial grounds. The fact that the general impression has always been that the agape was for memorials to the dead was perhaps the impression which the Christians wished to give to the authorities. If they were observing the Lord's Supper they could rightly claim that it was a memorial ceremony.

At Salina there are two agape tables so far discovered. Other catacombs in Malta have more than one also. That each is connected with the tombs close to it is the easiest assumption. Those catacombs without an agape would have to conduct their memorials on the flat tops of tombs. (There is a marked absence of any evidence of 'cataracts' or libation channels). The fact of agape tables reasonably close to each other could have another reason. Remembering the problem of persecution and the desire of Christians to meet together it would have been an advantage to have more than one agape table in a catacomb complex in order to vary the venue. They could thus avoid drawing attention to excessive regularity of meetings at the same spot. They could, in a sense, 'break bread from house to house' in an area somewhat short of available housing accommodation.

The hill in which the catacombs at Salina are cut is known

as il-Ghallis. Could this be derived from the days when Christians gathered around the agape earning for it the name of Chalice – the place of the cup?

The conclusion, then, that we reach from a study of the widespread tombs and catacombs in the Salina Bay area are that they are the burial places of the people of Beniarrad covering a period from before the arrival of Paul to a date near the end of Roman rule. There is evidence that the community became more and more Christianised and that forms of Christian worship were carried out here. Where the catacombs show signs of organisation they are likely to have been of a later date. There can be little doubt that somewhere in this area are the tombs of people who saw the shipwreck, met Paul and his fellow-travellers and treasured the memory of his visit.

Pottery sherds from each of the first five Christian centuries alongside tombs with symbols of the Christian religion bear witness to the fact that the ship wrecked but a few hundred yards away was a great turning point in the history of Maltà. Paul the prisoner came and left a faith.

CONCLUSION

The modern tourist relaxes in glorious sunshine, refreshes himself in the sparkling sea, is spellbound by the remarkable archaeological remains and the sheer architectural beauty of monument after monument. Those who pause to think see something deeper. They see a people who have survived the calamities which history has inflicted upon them as repeated waves of invasion came from every point of the compass. This island has always been the centre of the trade routes of the Mediterranean and the stepping stone between Europe and Africa. Both continents have claimed it in turn.

Blow after blow has tested the character. One by one the conquerors who jauntily strutted the rocky hills have had to depart. A kindly people have survived . . the Maltese. Their faith was founded upon a rock. With every disaster and heartbreak they have quietly set about the task of building again.

In AD60 the village folk emerged from their humble dwellings by the shore and helped the drenched and exhausted shipwreck survivors from the raging sea. They gave them warmth and food and shelter and opened their hearts and minds to a saintly messenger. Paul stayed for only three months but when he left there was a new spirit in an enchained generation which has never departed. So long as books are written and read this island will be remembered as a friendly refuge.

THE NARRATIVE

Acts of the Apostles

Ch. 27 When it was decided that we should sail to Italy, they handed Paul and some other prisoners over to Julius, an officer in the Roman army regiment called "The Emperor's Regiment." [2] We went aboard a ship from Adramyttium, which was ready to leave for the seaports of the province of Asia, and sailed away. Aristarchus, a Macedonian from Thessalonica, was with us. [3] The next day we arrived at Sidon. Julius was kind to Paul and allowed him to go and see his friends, to be given what he needed. [4] We went on from there, and because the winds were blowing against us we sailed on the sheltered side of the island of Cyprus. [5] We crossed over the sea off Cilicia and Pamphylia, and came to Myra, in Lycia. [6] There the officer found a ship from Alexandria that was going to sail for Italy, so he put us aboard.

[7] We sailed slowly for several days, and with great difficulty finally arrived off the town of Cnidus. The wind would not let us go any farther in that direction, so we sailed down the sheltered side of the island of Crete, passing by Cape Salmone. [8] We kept close to the coast, and with great difficulty came to a place called Safe Harbours, not far from the town of Lasea.

[9] We spent a long time there, until it became dangerous to continue the voyage, because by now the day of Atonement was already past. So Paul gave them this advice: [10] "Men, I see that our voyage from here on will be dangerous; there will be great damage to the cargo and to the ship, and loss of life as well." [11] But the army officer was convinced by what the captain and the owner of the ship said, and not by what

Paul said. [12] The harbour was not a good one to spend the winter in: so most of the men were in favour of putting out to sea and trying to reach Phoenix, if possible. It is a harbour in Crete that faces southwest and northwest, and they could spend the winter there.

[13] A soft wind from the south began to blow, and the men thought that they could carry out their plan; so they pulled up the anchor and sailed as close as possible along the coast of Crete. [14] But soon a very strong wind – the one called "Northeaster" – blew down from the island. [15] It hit the ship, and since it was impossible to keep the ship headed into the wind, we gave up trying and let it be carried along by the wind. [16] We got some shelter when we passed to the south of the little island of Cauda. There, with some difficulty, we managed to make the ship's boat secure. [17] They pulled it aboard, and then fastened some ropes tight around the ship. They were afraid that they might run into the sandbanks off the coast of Libya; so they lowered the sail and let the ship be carried by the wind. [18] The violent storm continued, so on the next day they began to throw the ship's cargo overboard, [19] and on the following day they threw the ship's equipment overboard with their own hands. [20] For many days we could not see the sun or the stars, and the wind kept on blowing very hard. We finally gave up all hope of being saved.

[21] After the men had gone a long time without food, Paul stood before them and said: "Men, you should have listened to me and not have sailed from Crete; then we would have avoided all this damage and loss. [22] But now I beg you, take courage! Not one of you will lose his life; only the ship will be lost. [23] For last night an angel of the God to whom I belong and whom I worship came to me [24] and said, 'Don't be afraid Paul! You must stand before the Emperor; and God, in his goodness, has given you the lives of all those who are sailing with you.' [25] And so, men, take courage! For I trust in God that it will be just as I was told. [26] But we will be driven ashore on some island.

[27] It was the fourteenth night, and we were being driven by the storm on the Mediterranean. About midnight the sailors suspected that we were getting close to land. [28] So they dropped a line with a weight tied to it and found that the

water was one hundred and twenty feet deep; a little later they did the same and found that it was ninety feet deep. [29] They were afraid that our ship would go on the rocks, so they lowered four anchors from the back of the ship and prayed for daylight. [30] The sailors tried to escape from the ship; they lowered the boat into the water and pretended that they were going to put out some anchors from the front of the ship. [31] But Paul said to the army officer and soldiers, "If these sailors don't stay on board, you cannot be saved." [32] So the soldiers cut the ropes that held the boat and let it go.

[33] Day was about to come, and Paul begged them all to eat some food: "You have been waiting for fourteen days now, and all this time you have not eaten a thing. [34] I beg you, then, eat some food; you need it in order to survive. Not even a hair of your heads will be lost." [35] After saying this, Paul took some bread, gave thanks to God before them all, broke it, and began to eat. [36] They took courage, and every one of them also ate some food. [37] There was a total of two hundred and seventy-six of us on board. [38] After everyone had eaten enough, they lightened the ship by throwing the wheat into the sea.

[39] When the day came, the sailors did not recognize the coast, but they noticed a bay with a beach and decided that, if possible, they would run the ship aground there. [40] So they cut off the anchors and left them in the water, and at the same time they untied the ropes that held the steering oars. Then they raised the sail at the front of the ship so that the wind would blow the ship forward, and headed for shore. [41] But the ship ran into a sandbank and went aground; the front part of the ship got stuck and could not move, while the back part was being broken to pieces by the violence of the waves.

[42] The soldiers made a plan to kill all the prisoners, so that none of them would swim ashore and escape. [43] But the army officer wanted to save Paul, so he stopped them from doing this. Instead, he ordered all the men who could swim to jump overboard first and swim ashore; [44] the rest were to follow, holding on to the planks or to some broken pieces of the ship. And this was how we all got safely ashore.

Ch. 28 When we were safely ashore, we learned that the island was called Malta. [2] The natives there were very friendly to us. It had started raining and was cold, so they built a fire and made us all welcome. [3] Paul gathered up a bundle of sticks and was putting them on the fire when a snake came out, on account of the heat, and fastened itself to his hand. [4] The natives saw the snake hanging on Paul's hand and said to one another, "This man must be a murderer, but Fate will not let him live, even though he escaped from the sea." [5] But Paul shook the snake off into the fire without being harmed at all. [6] They were waiting for him to swell up or suddenly fall down dead. But after waiting for a long time and not seeing anything unusual happening to him, they changed their minds and said, "He is a god!"

[7] Not far from that place were some fields that belonged to Publius, the chief of the island. He welcomed us kindly and for three days we were his guests. [8] Publius' father was in bed sick with fever and dysentery. Paul went into his room, prayed, placed his hands on him, and healed him. [9] When this happened, all the other sick people on the island came and were healed. [10] They gave us many gifts, and when we sailed they put on board what we needed for the voyage.

[11] After three months we sailed away on a ship from Alexandria, called "The Twin Gods," which had spent the winter in the island. [12] We arrived in the city of Syracuse and stayed there for three days. [13] From there we sailed on and arrived in the city of Rhegium. The next day a wind began to blow from the south, and in two days we came to the town of Puteoli. [14] We found some believers there who asked us to stay with them a week. And so we came to Rome. [15] The brothers in Rome heard about us and came as far as Market of Appius and Three Inns to meet us. When Paul saw them, he thanked God and took courage.

NOTES

1. (Pg 28) It is also noted that when a north east wind is blowing there is calmer water on the inner curve of Qawra.
2. (Pg 29) When, in 1963 he located the anchor stock near the entrance to Salina Bay Mr. Micallef-Borg was unable to shift it. He therefore asked the Navy for help with their lifting equipment. Subsequently it was stored at Manoel Island and was there until 1969. Other Roman anchor stocks found in Salina Bay are displayed at the National Museum, Valletta.
3. (Pg 44) 'Marcus Vallius, son of C. Vallius, patron of the Municipium, who had been knighted by Antonius Pius . . .'
4. (Pg 46) The cart ruts close to the Annunciata Chapel can be traced towards Naxxar for a considerable distance. In the field below the Lancer Hotel (which provides the best English style hotel food I have yet found) a set points towards San Pawl Milqi. Some one hundred and fifty yards ahead, very deeply cut, they continue through a farm and emerge behind the chapel of St. Michael where they disappear under the soil.
5. (Pg 48) The levels of the fields on each side of this road seem to indicate that it originally bordered the marsh of Roman days.
6. (Pg 49) 'Why Malta? Why Chawdex?' by D. Bellanti, Orphans' Press, see pages 24-30.
7. (Pg 50) Although spoiled by damage in removing the plaster which once covered it and later retouching this was obviously once a very beautiful portrait. The face has a haunting sadness.

   The enthusiastic piety of the lady at the church at Mellieha who explained the tradition to me and her parting words "You will always be welcome" was a true expression of Christianity at its best.
8. (Pg 57) See Acts of the Apostles Chapter 9.
9. (Pg 57) Towns in southern Turkey visited by Paul.
10. (Pg 57) See Acts of the Apostles Ch 15.
11. (Pg 58) See Acts of the Apostles Ch 22. v 18f.
12. (Pg 61) See 2. Timothy. Ch 4. v 13.
13. (Pg 64) Abbreviation of 1. Corinthians Ch 1. v 26.

14. (Pg 66) The present 2nd. century Theatre at Perga was built on the site of that in which Paul preached.

15. (Pg 69) See Acts of the Apostles Ch 19 v 29; 20, 4; 27, 2; Colossians 4, 10; Philemon 24.

16. (Pg 70) See Romans 16, 22.

17. (Pg 70) A convert who became a prominent church leader. See Galatians 2, 3; 2. Corinthians 2, 13; 7. 6 & 13; Epistle to Titus.

18. (Pg 71) The Acts of the Apostles was addressed to Theophilus.

19. (Pg 71) See 2. Timothy 4, 10.

20. (Pg 72) I have since learned that there is a very old tradition in Rabat linking Trophimus with Paul's stay in Malta and the association is with St. Paul's Grotto.

21. (Pg 90) Until recently little has been written about the Salina catacombs other than articles in the Times of Malta and a few paragraphs by D. H. Trump.

22. (Pg 94) Ancient Malta. Harrison Lewis. 1977.

23. (Pg 98) This carving appears to be either one which has been vandalised or an unfinished work. It is not mere graffiti but probably the earliest example of Christian art yet discovered in Malta. The grouping around the central figure gives the impression that the subject is the shipwrecked Paul being received and venerated by the people of Malta.

SELECTED BIBLIOGRAPHY

Ambrosini. M.L. 'The Secret Archives of the Vatican'. Eyre & Spotiswood 1970

Balsdon. J.P.V.D. 'Life & Leisure in Ancient Rome'. The Bodley Head. London

Bellanti. D. 'Why Malta? Why Chawdex?' Orphans Press, Chawdex

Bellanti. P.F. 'Studies in Maltese History'.

Beckwith. J. 'Early Christian and Byzantine Art.' Penguin Books Ltd. Middx. 1970

Bonnici. Mgr Prof. A. 'History of the Church in Malta Vol 1.' Empire Press, Catholic Institute 1967

Broadbent. E.H. 'The Pilgrim Church.' Pickering & Inglis Ltd. London

Bruce. F.F. 'New Testament History.' Thomas Nelson & Sons. London

'Paul'. The Paternoster Press. Exeter 1977

Burridge. W. 'Seeking the Site of St. Paul's shipwreck.' Progress Press Co Ltd, Valletta 1952

Casson. L. 'Travel in the Ancient World'. George Allen & Unwin London

Dibellius. M. 'Paul'. Longmans. London

Diess. J.J. 'Herculaneum' Souvenir Press. London

Filson. V.F. 'A New Testament History'. S.C.M. Press London

Finegan. J. 'Light from the Ancient Past.' Princeton University Press 1946

Franzan A./Dolan. J. 'Concise History of the Church'. Burns & Oats/London Herder & Herder 1969

Grant. M. 'Cities of Vesuvius (1971) 'The Jews in the Roman World' (1973)

'St. Paul'. Weidenfeld & Nicholson

Grant. R. 'Historical Introduction to the New Testament'. Collins. London. 1963

Green. M. 'Evangelism in the Early Church.' Hodder & Stoughton. London

Grimal. P. 'Civilization of Rome'. George Allen & Unwin Ltd. London 1963

Gunton. L. 'Rome's Historic Churches'. George Allen & Unwin London 1969
Johnson. P. 'A History of Christianity'. Weidenfeld & Nicholson London
Josephus 'The Jewish War'. Penguin Classics. London.
Kelly. J.N.D. 'Early Christian Creeds.' Longmans. London. 1950
Kinninmonth. C. 'Travellers Guide to Malta.' Johnathan Cape. London 1967
Lewis. H. 'Ancient Malta'. Colin Smythe. Bucks 1977
Lindsay. J. 'Leisure & Pleasure in Roman Egypt'. Frederick Muller Ltd. London 1965
MacMullen. R. 'Constantine'. Weidenfeld & Nicholson. London 1970
Meiggs. R. 'Roman Ostia'. Clarenden Press. 1973
Parker. J. 'The Foundations of Judaism & Christianity.' Valentine-Mitchell. London 1960
Perowne. S. 'Caesars & Saints'. Hodder & Stoughton. London 1962
Pollock. J. 'The Apostle'. Hodder & Stoughton. 1969
Rahner. H. 'Green Myths & Christian Mysteries'. Burns & Oats. London 1963
Raven. S. 'Rome in Africa'. Evans Brothers Ltd. London 1969
Rops. H. D. 'Daily Life in Palestine at the time of Christ'. Weidenfeld & Nicholson. 1962
Robertson. A. 'The Origins of Christianity.' Lawrence & Wishart. London. 1954
Salmon. E.T. 'History of the Roman World 30BC – AD138'. Methuen & Co Ltd. London
Schonfield. H. 'Those Incredible Christians'. Hutchinson. London 1968
'For Christ's Sake'. Macdonald & Janes London
'The Jew of Tarsus'. Macdonald & Janes. 1946
Smith. J. 'The Voyage & Shipwreck of St. Paul'. Collins 1948
Smith. M. 'The Secret Gospel'. Victor Gollanz. London.
Streeter. B.H. 'The Primitive Church'. Macmillan. London 1929
Toynbee. J.M.C. 'Death & Burial in the Roman World.' Thames & Hudson. London
Trump. D.H. 'Malta: An Archaeological Guide'. Faber & Faber London 1972